# Dear Her...

Letters to Teenage Girls and Young Ladies About
Lessons Learned Through Education, Athletics, and Life

by Leslie Trujillo, Deanna Cordova, Kimberly Jones
and Amazing Contributing Women

Foreword by Nicole Ari Parker

# ABOUT THE COVER

(Cover Artwork by Lucinda Rudolph)

## *THE STORY OF THE BUTTERFLY*

A young girl was playing outside and found an amazing caterpillar. She picked it up and took it home to show her family. She asked if she could keep it, and they said she could if she would take good care of it.

The girl got a large jar from her mother and put plants in it for the caterpillar to eat. Every day she watched the caterpillar and brought it new plants. One day the caterpillar started acting weird. The girl worriedly called her mother, who came and understood that the caterpillar was creating a cocoon. The mother explained to the girl how the caterpillar was going to go through a metamorphosis and soon become a butterfly.

The little girl was thrilled to hear about the changes her caterpillar would go through. She watched every day, waiting for the butterfly to emerge. One day it happened; a small hole appeared in the cocoon and the butterfly started to struggle to come out.

At first the girl was excited, but soon she became worried. The butterfly was struggling so hard to get out! It looked like it could not break free and needed help. It didn't seem to be making any progress. The girl was so concerned, she decided to help. She went to get scissors. She snipped the cocoon to make the hole bigger and the butterfly quickly emerged.

As the butterfly came out, the girl was surprised. It had a swollen body and small, shriveled wings. She continued to watch the butterfly, expecting that at any moment the wings would enlarge and expand to support the swollen body. She knew that the body would eventually shrink and the butterfly's wings would grow; however, neither happened! The butterfly spent the rest of its life crawling around with a swollen body and shriveled wings. It never was able to fly...

The girl talked to a scientist to find out what went wrong. She learned that the butterfly was **SUPPOSED** to struggle. In fact, the butterfly's struggle to push its way through the tiny opening of the cocoon pushes the fluid out of its body and into its wings. Without the struggle, the butterfly would never, ever fly. The girl's good intentions hurt the butterfly. The struggling is an important part of any growth experience. **The struggle is where you develop and find your strength to fly.**

## *THE STORY OF THE CHINESE BAMBOO*

The parable of the Chinese Bamboo Tree teaches us lessons about faith, growth, development, patience, perseverance, and the journey of our potential. Like any plant, the Chinese Bamboo Tree requires nurturing–water, fertile soil and sunshine to grow. In the first year, there are no visible signs of activity or development. In the second year, again, no growth above the soil. And the third and fourth, still no signs. Patience is tested and we begin to wonder if our efforts will ever be rewarded because we are not seeing the growth above soil.

Finally, in the fifth year, there is growth...and it is amazing growth! The Chinese Bamboo Tree grows around 80 feet in just six weeks above the ground! How is that possible?

What happened in the first five years was not that the tree was not growing—it was growing! It was developing a strong root system and growing underground. The growth needed to be deep first to develop a strong foundation to support the big upward growth that was to come. It also needed to develop its strength to handle whatever winds and storms may attack the bamboo in the future. The roots sustain the growth.

The Chinese Bamboo Tree is a perfect parable to our own experience of personal growth and development. **Continue to have faith as you work toward your vision and dreams. Have patience and perseverance as you develop your strong roots.**

# ABOUT THE SYMBOL IN THE BOOK BETWEEN THE LETTERS

## *THE STORY OF THE LOTUS FLOWER*

The lotus flower is one of the most remarkable creations of nature. Its beauty lies in its purity, because this magnificent flower emerges from the dirty and muddy bottom of a pond yet remains untouched and unstained by its soiled surroundings. The lotus flower is regarded in many different cultures as a symbol of **purity, enlightenment, strength, grace, beauty, self-regeneration and rebirth**. Its characteristics are a perfect analogy for the human condition; even when its roots are in the dirtiest waters, the lotus produces the most beautiful flower.

# Letters From

Dear Her ...Your struggle will become your strength. Without struggle, a butterfly could not grow strong enough to take flight!

This book is dedicated to all the females who have struggled in some area of their life. May you continue to develop your roots, grow in your journey and strengthen your wings to fly!

You are beautiful and the world needs you ...

# FOREWORD

Since before Abraham, Jesus, Cleopatra or Tutankhamen ... since before T-Rex or Lucy the Australopithecus, there has always been TROUBLE. Seismic shifts, weather conditions, betrayal, fate, famine, desire and war have been the same issues everyone had to face, all over the world, century after century, forever. There is just no getting around it ... Winter is always coming!

So is the rain,

And the first kiss,

A funeral,

A slipped disk,

A pimple,

And an offensive foul.

The stuff that happens to us varies from person to person. They can range from the "Pssht, I moved on from that, no problem" category to the "almost ruined my life."

How did I recover from seeing my first boyfriend kissing someone else?

How did I arrive at NYU at seventeen and survived NYC for thirteen years?

How did I literally do my absolute best, gave it my all, practiced and prayed to make the cut and .... Wait ... I didn't make it? Wait, what? How?

How did I manage to start a business with two small kids?

The "Offensive Fouls" can also seem insurmountable and devastating.

How did my husband's grandmother survive Nazi Germany with three children?

How did my mom survive the deep south as a little girl in the 1940s and '50s? How did she buy her ice chips and soda in the hot summer at the back door of the "nice people" ice cream parlor when Woolworths wouldn't serve her at all? How did she walk home sometimes seeing people being untied from trees where their lives had been taken? How did she live through that, THEN raise a daughter to love all people?

How did my dad grow up in abject poverty in the inner city of Baltimore, shined shoes and stacked bowling pins at 12-years-old to help his mom after his father died, then later drive a taxi to put himself through school to become a dentist? And all before he had a right to vote. How?

HOW?

I think there is a moment in everyone's life when they have to make the decision that their inner life, their inner self-talk, their inner mental strength is more important than the outer messages, no matter how strong and convincing the messages are.

Sometimes people are born with this ability. They are raised in unimaginable adversity or with a mountain of setbacks in their backpack, with the whole ENTIRE world pushing against them, and still somehow their courageous spirit boils up inside them. Their will to live and their determination to love drowns out the noise and informs everything they do. These people have no other option than to keep going. Yes, they were afraid ... but they did it anyway. These are often our grandparents. Their natural strength kept them here, which, by the way of their survival, brought us here.

Some people, in adverse situations or not, are consciously empowered by family or teachers or coaches who do their best, who think of every positive lesson, inside and out, that they can give their children and students. These children then take these blessings and grow up to become beacons of light and hope to others on their path.

Some people, like most of us, and like our daughters and sons today, are relentlessly inundated by exterior distorted messages and experiences very early in life, often so fast there is no time for anyone to catch it. Then we are told to "make it happen" without any awareness of the power and beauty and magnificence already "happening" inside of us. Everyone is just managing. Maybe our families believed, "My kids are good, responsible … they got this. No problem." With so much coming at everyone, so much pressure and not enough time, a decision is quickly made to be realistic and focus more on the outside rules, thinking that would help them most in the real world:

"Get good grades.

Keep your head up.

Follow the rules.

Work hard.

Save your money.

Make us proud."

They were right. What happens, however, is that when you do not have another set of empowering inner rules firmly in place, when the proverbial asteroid hits the dinosaur, your "spiritual toolkit" comes up empty—or you do not even know you had one. This is where a book like DEAR HER comes in. Its pages are full of reminders of who we are and what we are capable of. It also lets us know how important it is to develop the inner self-care muscle when navigating through life, no matter where you are on the path.

Someone once asked me, "Would you like to be friends with someone who talked to you the way you talk to yourself?" I was stunned. I quickly replayed in my head the last round of thoughts I had in my head ... those soft whispers of negativity that often feel like protection and preparation.

"Are you really going to wear that?

Well, it's all I've got!

Don't!

Doesn't matter.

I should have done more to get ahead.

I should have gone to the parties.

I didn't know all this other stuff mattered.

What is wrong with your voice?

You can't sing.

Just don't say anything.

Why am I here?

People look at me weird.

I can't stay here long.

I can just be by myself.

I like being alone anyway.

Ugh, I hate people.

I wish I hadn't come here.

I'm not pretty.

Who cares?

Pretty doesn't matter.

Smart matters.

Dumb matters, too, apparently.

What am I doing wrong?

I'm missing something.

I'm not cut out for this."

I had to laugh, because I had all the thought options in the world, and this is what I wasted 30 seconds on. Which, of course, turned into minutes, hours, and days …

Uh, no! This friendship with "Negative Nancy" would not last very long. However, I lived with lists like this forever. As time went on and I became a wife and mother, the lists got more layered and clever and debilitating. I had two negative responses to every positive one and just spent years cancelling myself out. I held on to the words of my parents when I could …

"If you fall down, get back up."

"You can do it."

"I believe in you."

These words kept me afloat, but just like your free throws and penalty kicks, you have to PRACTICE your inner life, too. More specifically, you have to DECIDE to practice, because, well, you are going to need it.

Sometimes this decision takes you by surprise. Sometimes a tool is dropped in your lap and the DECISION MAKES YOU. A few years ago, I was sitting in the makeup room getting prepped to shoot a scene for a television show. I was feeling quite self-conscious about everything, from the small part I was playing for no money at this point in my career, to my looks, to being away from my kids for hours and hours ... days, even. At some point, I just looked at the corner of the mirror in front of me and saw a note the hairdresser had written and taped to the glass:

"Is it KIND ... is it NECESSARY ... is it TRUE?"

Hmmm. "What is that?" I asked.

She replied, "Sometimes when I have a strong thought or opinion that I'm about to elaborate on, share with someone else, believe about myself or just let sink in, I ask myself, "Is this kind, necessary, or true?"

I was blown away, not only by the beauty of these words, but also by the fact that she had a moment-to-moment practice, a gentle tool that empowered her in the face of all that was coming at her and coming *from* her AND that she put it in a place where she could share it with others.

That is exactly what DEAR HER is; a group of women who gathered their tools, put them in a place where others can see them, and turned on the light bulb of decision. Their voices are passionate, strong, and experienced. As I turned each page, I was so grateful for these women sharing their stories. I drank in all the new ideas they live by and all the old ones I could feel the ancestors passed along. I wanted to start a daily practice again, I wanted to write the empowering sentences down over and over. I wanted to read them out loud. I could feel them taking up space in my mind and in my heart. I wanted to wake up my 13-year-old daughter and read these essays to her. I wanted to listen to her and see where she may have wasted some seconds to let in some unkind, unnecessary, and untrue thoughts; and then find a way to ease them out.

Remember to...

Fail forward.

Be present.

Gratitude changes everything.

Trust in your ability to figure things out.

You are more than a label.

Never forget you are a miracle.

Plant powerful seeds.

Be afraid and do it anyway!

My DEAR HER, you will be ready for the world. For the Winter and the Spring, for the first love or the torn meniscus, for the trial and the triumph ... for IT ALL!

All my love to you,

*Nicole Ari Parker*

## About Nicole Ari Parker

Nicole Ari Parker is a seven-time NAACP Image Award nominee known for her role on Showtime's award-winning series, "Soul Food". She graduated from NYU's famed Tisch School of the Arts and has appeared on Broadway, the big screen and on television. Parker currently stars as Giselle on the Fox series, "EMPIRE". She lives in California with her husband, Boris Kodjoe, their two children and their dog Max. Together they founded the Kodjoe Family Foundation and the high-performance fitness headband The GYMWRAP.

# Introduction

This book is a reminder to you of your worth, beauty, and strength. It has come from a lifetime of women's journeys. It is a reminder that you are not alone. Anything that you are going through, there is probably someone in the world who has gone through a similar situation and made it through stronger than they were before. Let these letters help you understand that you can make it through any challenge in front of you. Allow them to also remind you to celebrate yourself and enjoy the journey; everything in your life is happening for you. We do not know all the answers. All we know is that we can share our experiences with you and have compassion for ourselves as we journey down our paths together.

Let us start with the truth. You are enough. You are loved. Let those two sentences really sink in. You are enough. You are loved. Say those two sentences to yourself and feel it to be true. In the end, it all comes down to the words you say to yourself. Those words are more important than any words that would come from another person. It took me a long time to understand that to be true for myself. I struggled with my self-esteem and believing in myself when I was younger. My parents always told me that I was enough, and I was loved, but I thought they had to tell me that because they were my parents, so I did not believe it. I was under the illusion that something in my life—or I—needed to be a little different before I would be happy. It was a never-ending feeling of "not being good enough."

I would like to tell you a little about my journey and how this idea of the book came to be. I was a happy and outgoing little girl, full of life and confidence. I do not remember when exactly that changed, but I remember sometime around 3rd grade starting to feel more concerned about what others thought of me and that I was not good enough. We had moved states and I had to make new friends. I was full of fear on the inside but tried to act tough on the outside. I remember feeling different because I had to leave my normal class to go to speech therapy and "enrichment." I had glasses and braces at a time when not a lot of kids had them. I did not like being different. I was overweight as well, and the boys would tease me. Around the 6th grade, my parents separated, and I was full of anger and sadness. I held all my frustrations inside and did not want to talk about my feelings. I was mean to my younger sister and my parents because of my hurt. I did not understand that these were outside circumstances and it was how I chose to interpret those events inside me that created my pain. My perceptions, which were distorted, became my reality. Everyone thought I was happy and strong because I showed that person to the outside world, but inside I was full of doubt and fear.

The only escape I had from my feelings was sports. Athletics and staying active were my outlet. When my love of sports was threatened by a negative coach, I felt defeated. I felt lost. I did not know how to navigate through life and sports. I shared my dreams and goals with my coach, and she laughed at me. Never let anyone steal your joy or believe them when they say you cannot have a dream. They do not know what you are made of deep inside or how important that dream is to you. I made the decision right there that I was going to go after my dream with all my energy, and even if it did not happen, I knew I would be stronger for trying. I also decided that I would never laugh at someone else's dream. I wanted to empower others along their journey.

When I stopped playing sports in college, I struggled with my identity. Who was I, if I was not an athlete anymore? It was a dark and depressing time for me, and I turned to alcohol. That just led to more problems and the loss of my sense of self-worth. I never knew how powerful alcohol could be or that it could take over my life. It was not until I almost died from drinking that I paused to look at my life and asked myself, "What are you doing and how are you living?" I reached out for help and found strength through other women that made it through similar struggles to those I had experienced. They brought me back to life and helped me find my strength.

It has been a journey of growth. I have watched my sister, Deanna, grow through many different struggles and celebrations of her own. My friend, Kim, shared her challenges and opportunities with us and we found strength by sharing with each other. We decided that we wanted young girls to know that they are not alone. We wanted to give them the awareness of how powerful they are in navigating life's journey. Although the different hardships in our lives felt like they were happening *to* us we did not understand that they were actually happening *for* us. They were calling to us to rise up, to become the strong women we are meant to be.

I thought of this book idea around ten years ago. I shared it with a group of women when I was onstage at a business event. I then got busy with building my career, getting married, becoming a mom, so much so that I forgot about this book idea. Last year, I was at a parent-teacher event and the English teacher, Ms. Lilly Hodges, asked us to write a letter to the seniors on our advice we would give them about their senior year. I thought that was a great idea! That inspired me to take action with Deanna and Kim to collect letters and put this book together. I totally forgot that I originally had this idea ten years ago, until I saw a video clip of that Ali Brown event. Let that be a reminder to you that sometimes things that you want do not happen immediately, or at the specific time you think it will, but if you continue to work on yourself and trust the universe, it will happen in an even better time or in a better way. The idea was in my heart, but I had more growth to do, more experiences to have, more people to meet. Trust the timing to unfold in the proper way. Understand that process as you work on your goals and dreams.

This book will benefit any young girl and even grown women; however, we particularly wanted to write this book to young student-athletes for several reasons:

1) We were all student-athletes ourselves and know the highs and lows that come through athletics.

2) We love sports and the lessons it has taught us that have guided us in life.

3) We are coaches and have worked with thousands of young athletes and seen challenges and triumphs they have gone through in their life.

4) A lot of our athletes believe we are strong women and role models, but do not realize we were just like them once and have struggles in our lives, too.

5) Girls and women sometimes think we are in competition with one another, instead of understanding that we need to collaborate with one another, because our strength lies in our community and building each other up.

6) We believe there is so much power in a group of women coming together, and that is exactly what our world needs right now. Even if you are not an athlete, and you choose to be creative through the arts or music, there will be encouragement in these letters for you.

Throughout our journey of struggles and celebrations, we have learned a lot of lessons that we want to share with you to help you along your own life's journey. We asked several of our friends to share their wisdom so you can see the variety of experiences and know that you are not alone. No matter what you have gone through, are going through currently, or will go through in the future, most likely someone else has also experienced that and can help you along the way.

In life, you are going to have different experiences in school, athletics, activities, work, and relationships. Remember that it all starts with knowing you have all the beauty, strength, courage, and wisdom within you to shine. You just need to continue to believe and surround yourself with positive friends, family, and mentors who empower you. It is about learning and growing; whatever you are going through will pass, so enjoy the great times and find your strength in the tough times. And never give your power away to another!

Following are letters from women on what they would write to their younger selves or to another young lady. There are several ways you can read this book:

1. You can read the book straight through.

2. You can read one letter a day.

3. You can randomly flip through the book and stop on a page and read that letter that day.

Whatever you decide, enjoy!

P.S. Each letter is the personal belief and experience of each woman. There may be various opinions and views amongst the letters. We wanted to show how we are all unique and wise. What works for one person might not work for another, but it is important to be open and respect each person as they share their life with us.

P.P.S. The importance of this project can be summarized from an excerpt from "*The Awakened Woman*" by Dr. Tererai Trent:

"*Other women's successful actions are not your competition, they are your inspiration and your opportunities. Sometimes the best way to overcome our own silencing is to see how others are rising above theirs. When we truly understand other women's journeys, the contours their paths take, the steep climb and the silent terrain that becomes more visible when we share them, we can know for sure that we will also make it. We need the wisdom of those who have traveled the same path: these women pathfinders, the torch bearers, the ones who have been silenced but have found their redemption against all odds, claimed their own voices and then remembered those left behind.*"

## DEAR HER,

Hello, Beautiful! I hope you know how beautiful and amazing you really are in every way! When I was young, I didn't realize that, because I didn't look like what the media and society portrayed to be "beautiful." I judged myself as ugly, all wrong, and made myself less than all my peers. I didn't think I was good enough, smart enough, or pretty enough to ever be happy and successful. The truth is, those are outside things that are temporary and transform as you grow, but they will never define who you are, so please do not let any labels block your beauty from shining.

**YOU:** You are unique! No one else has the same fingerprints, footprints, talents, dreams, experiences, personality, and combination of all of those that you do. Know that you are special and have many gifts to offer the world. Cherish yourself and follow your dreams in all that you do. Do not waste energy comparing yourself to anyone else.

**DREAMS:** If you have a dream or desire for something, you must pay attention to it and care for it. It is yours for a reason. It is usually calling you to grow and develop through the fulfillment of your dream. Do everything in your power to work for it. Seek coaching, ask for help, and do something every day that moves you forward. Do not pay attention to anyone who tells you that it's not possible; it's your dream, not theirs. They do not know the power within you to accomplish what you want. Continue to work for it, and even if it does not turn out the way you wanted it to, you will have become stronger in the pursuit and find a different reward. It is in the pursuit where the dream comes alive.

**FEAR:** Do not let fear dominate or control you. It is your companion. Fear will always show up in different areas of your life; use it to push you forward to the next level of your life. If you face the fear, you will grow out of your comfort zone to develop. It is okay to be afraid, just don't let it get in your way.

**SCHOOL:** Value the opportunities to grow your mind. Every time you focus, comprehend, analyze, and learn something new, your brain grows new neural connections. This empowers your brain to be stronger to handle situations in all areas of your life. Seek the learning experience, not necessarily just the grade. It's great to reach for A's, but don't let that define you. Let the effort and learning be your focus.

Did you give your best in each class, despite the subject, teacher, or grasp of the subject? Show up every day, do your homework right away, plan when you are going to study, and approach each assignment and test with confidence, knowing you did all you could to prepare. Everything is a skill. If you approach school this way, it will cross over to sports and other areas of life.

**COACHES:** We all have had different experiences with coaches. I have had very negative coaches who took away my passion for my sport and I have had amazing coaches who challenged and pushed me to improve every day. No matter what type of coach you have, know they are doing the best they can, and they have put in a lot of time and effort to coach you. Appreciate them. Use their coaching and feedback to fuel your passion and build you up. All you can control is the effort you give on every play. Do not worry about your playing time or mistakes you make, just be prepared to give your best when it's your time. After every practice, after every game, thank your coach—even when you don't feel like it.

**TEAMMATES:** Your teammates are your family. There is a strong bond and sisterhood that gets created fighting along your journey or your season. They were with you through all the sweat, tears, and celebrations. Remember, you are not competing against them; you are competing with them.

Competition means to bring out the best in another. That is your job; you need to make your teammates better by holding them accountable and pushing them to be their best. When the season is over, every single teammate played an important role. Everyone contributed. Whether you play every minute in a game or you never get in, your energy and effort matter! Every day you give your best and build a more solid foundation together for tomorrow. Because they are like your family and you are with them a lot, there may be times when you argue or irritate each other. Learn to communicate and let it go. It's not worth the negative energy. Don't bully anyone, or have "cliques" within your team; it will hurt the power of the group. Always think about what's best for your team and how you can work together. These are skills that will last a lifetime.

**COMPETITION:** Why do you compete? What comes from it? It's not about the W's and L's, it's about how you show up and how you grow through the competition. Always remember: You give 100 percent to prepare for the battle, and when it's game time, you show up mentally and physically ready to give it your all. It doesn't matter the circumstances, if you're tired, sick, have other distractions going on in your life—you show up focused and driven. Give your best on every play with intention and passion. Be aggressive, take risks, and play to win. Don't play to not make mistakes, or with concern of what others will say—play your game. It's about the energy you bring, your demeanor of confidence and drive. When you're ahead, keep going hard and take care of the fundamentals. Don't let up and stop doing what got you the lead. Complacency and arrogance are your enemies. When you're behind, never give up. Keep attacking play by play; you can't score ten points at once. Just keep chipping away and keep the faith. You're never alone. Your coaches, teammates, and family are there to help you throughout the journey. Ask for help when you need it and be the spark for them when they need it. AND ONE MORE THING—this isn't just about sports, this is about life. Seek out the best competition to push you to a higher level, welcome the struggle, stay the course, and you will develop into not only a Champion of Sport, but a Champion of Life!

**FAMILY:** I never valued my family in high school. I didn't like the rules and discipline they enforced. Looking back, those rules were not even severe, they were just guidelines to help me be considerate of my family. My perception was way off. I didn't realize how much they sacrificed and worked hard to give me many opportunities in academics, athletics and life. I never thanked them enough. Whatever your family dynamic, know you are loved. I argued with my little sister all the time, but now she is my best friend. It took me growing up to realize how important they are to me in every area of my life. Help them out whenever you can and spend quality time talking with them. Tell them thank you and that you love them as much as you can. More importantly, show them your love and gratitude.

**INJURY:** When you play hard and compete, there is always a chance that you may sustain an injury. No matter how positive a person you are, you will feel down and discouraged at first. It's okay to be sad and disappointed, but just don't stay in that state too long. Your body and mind are extremely powerful. You might be back sooner than you know. Do everything your doctors, physical therapists, athletic trainers, coaches, and parents tell you to do about resting and rehabbing. You can control how much sleep you get and the foods you eat. Great nutrition and solid sleep are key to recovery. Visualize your body healing and you performing again with strength. Stay with the team as much as you can: go to practices, travel with the team, and attend every game. Give your best energy and support to your team. Visualize yourself performing. Have faith in the process and know that you will come back stronger than before, emotionally, mentally, and physically. When you return, there is always a chance of another injury, but don't let fear hold you back. Know that you are more powerful than any circumstance. You are more than an athlete. Keep pressing forward in a goal that moves your soul.

**HEALTH:** The best athletes are well-fueled and well-rested. Make sure you are eating breakfast, lunch, dinner, and snacks before and after practice. You need good protein, healthy fat, veggies, and fruit. Minimize processed and junk food. They call it that for a reason. When you put garbage into your body, the output of performance is garbage. Minimize wasted time on your phone and front of the television so you can go to bed as early as possible. Anything after 10:30 begins to interfere with your recovery time.

**DRUGS & ALCOHOL:** Despite what people might tell you or how "fun" they say it is, alcohol and drugs will do absolutely nothing to move you forward to your dreams and goals. As a matter of fact, it will slowly or quickly take you far away. Physiologically, it gets in the way of your muscular development and contractions, slowing you down. It gets in the way of your regeneration and recovery. Alcohol and drugs kill brain cells and will interfere with learning new plays, making decisions in your sport, and disrupt memory. It will not only get in the way of sports, but it will affect your education and relationships as well. Your frontal lobe of your brain doesn't fully develop until you are 25, so any substance you take before then is going to interfere with your decision making. Stay alert, stay healthy, stay committed to your development and don't let anything get in the way of your advancement.

**TRUTH:** Stay true to yourself. Listen to your intuition. Don't let anyone force you into doing something that does not feel right to you. There is a knowledge, a truth within you that will guide you. Be still and listen. It's easy to get distracted by all the noise of social media and listening to what all your peers are doing but stay true to you and your voice.

Through it all, you are going to have wins and you will have some losses. You are going to laugh, and you are going to cry. You are going to feel like you belong, and you are going to feel alone. Don't be so hard on yourself; we are all a work in progress, there is no perfection. No matter what, seek the challenge and honor the struggle because YOUR STRUGGLE WILL BECOME YOUR STRENGTH!

Stay strong and love always,

*Leslie "Coach C" Trujillo*

P.S. Lessons I learned from playing tennis for UNM Lobos:

1) Even when you don't believe in yourself, there is someone else who does, so believe in their belief in you!

2) My dad called the coach (Kathy Kolanciewicz) and said I wanted to try out. I had no idea he called, and I even didn't know I wanted to play—when you get a call back or an opportunity, even when you're scared—take it!

3) Never listen to people who tell you you're not good enough to play at the next level; instead listen to the ones who tell you, "you can have the opportunity if you're willing to work hard for it and dedicate yourself 100 percent"

4) Work with the coaches who push you every day and challenge you to grow. They will give you all the tools, you just need to listen and apply them to every area of your life.

5) Focus on the Process. I decided to redshirt my freshman year and didn't compete in matches, but I improved the most and won the "Spirit Award" for the energy and support I brought to the team. You always have something to give!

6) You elevate your game when you surround yourself with people who are also committed to be their best. Your environment is key to growth.

7) Even when you're finished playing, the lessons you learned will never leave you. The countless hours you dedicated to your sport give you the foundation to apply to any dream or goal you have.

8) You will always be an athlete. Life is the most competitive sport of all; bring the passion and focus into your life.

9) Utilize your experience and knowledge to give back and help others. The lessons I learned from playing sports have fueled my passion & philosophy for training champions for over 18 years.

10) Be grateful for it all. Appreciate the journey. Then reach back and inspire another.

# DEAR HER,

You are probably too young to understand this, but decisions that you have made plague me to this day. At the same time, it is those same decisions that I once assumed led me down the wrong path that have brought me to where I am right now. I believed for years that what I was experiencing was regret based on "poor" decisions you made. But really, when I look back, you were the brave one. You didn't pursue collegiate basketball and you quit that club basketball team that was ranked nationally because you were too intimidated by the competition. Well, let me tell you, I train athletes all the time that aren't committed to the process. I can tell their hearts aren't in it. Maybe they're playing because their parents are making them or because it was expected of them. I'm not sure, but sometimes I think that would have been you had you decided to play college ball or stay on that club basketball team. It takes courage to do what you did. It wasn't for you, and instead of being passive-aggressive, you made difficult decisions to walk away.

You have no idea how motivated I have become as an adult because of those two critical decisions. I understand that you didn't have the confidence to take a leap of faith, but that is okay. You weren't ready to. You will when you're older, and I am living proof. It's okay that you weren't able to challenge yourself and step into discomfort. You should know that you would have been fine if you had, but you had to learn those skills later in life. I need you to understand that there is a difference between failing and being a failure. You are not a failure because you made those decisions. Life has a way of working itself out, and let's just say things worked out. Everything is happening at the right time and at the right pace. I'm right where I need to be in life and so are you. Instead of focusing on a specific destination, just sit back and enjoy the ride. The fun is in the journey, and you are missing it while you stress about the future. Life at your age should have been a lot easier than you made it. Every decision you make is the right one, so stop fretting. The repercussions, whether they are good or bad, will teach you valuable lessons. They will prepare you for anything that life throws your way. There are no mistakes, just opportunities for growth. Be still and appreciate what you have right this minute and at this precise moment in time.

The reason I got into bodybuilding is because of you and those same decisions you made regarding basketball. The competitive bug bit me later in life and it is a direct reflection of the decision to not play ball at an elite level. Not playing college hoops also meant that I had to find a way to stay in shape. My passion for fitness and health began the moment I made the decision to discontinue organized ball. I changed my eating habits and took initiative to lose weight and stay in shape. After spending most of my life participating in organized practice for dance or basketball, I had to start scheduling my own fitness routine. You did this PRE-INTERNET! You didn't have any online workouts or Instagram videos available to learn about nutrition and health. You just figured it out and took it upon yourself to put your health in your hands. You have no idea how proud I am of you. I don't know if I could stand here now at the age of 38 and say I would have had a successful professional career, with 16 years of experience in the fitness industry and ten years in collegiate-level strength and conditioning, if it hadn't been for your decision to do what was in your heart. I stopped beating myself up about those decisions years ago once I realized how valuable they were to the person I am today.

Thoughts are very powerful, but negative thoughts about yourself will torture you. Make it a priority to get out of your head. Get a head start on that now and you will save yourself years of unnecessary fear, shame and suffering. You take life so seriously—if you could let go of the constant chatter in your head that isn't productive, I promise that you will relax into a new reality that is so much more fun and rewarding. Don't trip. I am still working on this now. The key word is WORK. It's a daily practice, but trust me when I tell you that I know how damaging insecurities are. You were such an outgoing kid before puberty hit, and that same confident kid is still inside of you. Accept yourself for who you are, stop comparing yourself to others and she will re-emerge. You will never look like all the girls that you envy. You're not supposed to. You are beautiful on your best days and even more stunning on your worst. Your flaws do not define you. They are merely reflections of brief moments in time when you have lost sight of your greatness. They are reminders that you will stumble from time to time. So, when you say hurtful things to others, gossip, or take people you care about for granted, don't beat yourself up about it. Reflect on your actions and forgive yourself. No more obsessing or over-analyzing! Clear your mind and be in the present. Forgive others as well. Harboring resentment towards people just to make a point is a waste of energy. Being a Scorpio is no longer an excuse for cutting people off in your life. You're going to find that forgiveness is probably one of the most powerful feelings in the world. Don't judge others, be compassionate and respond with love even when it is not being shown towards you. When you do this, your authentic self will shine through. Let me tell you, this will feel so rewarding. Being filled with positive energy is far more enjoyable then emanating hate and angst. Positive thoughts attract positive things into your life. They will manifest in wonderful blessings that keep your mind at ease. Negative thoughts will attract negative things into your life and keep you in a holding pattern that won't let you escape the flood of negative emotions.

Revel at the opportunities you are given every day to achieve true happiness. This means you need to start opening up. When you hold in your feelings and suppress your emotions, you bottle up your potential for growth. Allow yourself to feel every emotion within the wide spectrum of your inner sentiments. Your ego will fight you on this, so be strong, girl! Ditch the distractions so you can look inside yourself. Investigate and look around. That means cut the TV off right now! Actually, unplug it, and store it in the garage. It's rotting your brain. It's distracting you from focusing on yourself. Escaping into the world of TV won't remove the feelings of rejection, anxiety and low self-esteem. You're experiencing a wide range of emotions right now, and it's imperative that you sit with them. Don't deny them nor disregard them. They are valuable teachers. Explore your inner self and acknowledge the beauty in everything that you find. That means love yourself and believe that you are also worthy of receiving love.

## TOUGH LOVE TIME:

- No more supersize meals from here on out. You'll thank me when you're older. Two words: Chronic Inflammation. Look it up.

- You're not allergic to books—start reading. The knowledge I have now about meditation, shame, vulnerability, energy and vibrational forces have saved my life. Get your ass in the library. It will be your one-way ticket toward enlightenment.

- Let me tell you something about the ego. It is vicious. It will infiltrate your mind and thoughts, spewing discouraging statements like, "you aren't pretty enough, thin enough, talented enough or smart enough to succeed." Let those thoughts pass through your body like a cold chill. They aren't true, so pay them no attention. Once you start believing in yourself, they will be easier to ignore. Whether you agree with it or not, accept what's happening in the present. When you fight it, it will make your life unbearable. Let go and let flow. Release any apprehensions you have about your current situation, otherwise stress and anxiety will devour your spirit. Reality is always a beautiful thing. Life happens whether you relinquish control or not, so roll with it and discover how easy it can be when you don't feel tortured and powerless. Your power lies within when your faith is strong. Faith fosters peace. Fear casts a wide net of devastation. Every day that you are fortunate to wake up is beautiful.

— Stop settling. Be great and respect the work that must be put in to achieve greatness. PUT. IN. THAT. WORK! Do your homework and stop copying your way through school. Information is your salvation. High school is literally just time management. You're spending way too much time on the telephone and watching TV, and not nearly enough time study-ing and doing homework. FOCUS. Apply yourself. You're not dumb, you're just not trying. Stop cheat-ing and start changing. Academic success scares you because it would mean you care about school. It's okay if you do and it's not cool to pretend you don't.

— Stop being so entrenched with your physical char-acteristics. People don't view you as negatively as you view yourself. Shift the focus from your outer appearance and enrich your soul, young lady. You'll be able to attract all those blessings that you're longing for when you do. Beat me to the chase and enhance your mind on these topics now. It will save you decades of unnecessary suffering. I love you. I love everything about you, and one day you will, too.

Love,

*Kim Jones*

## DEAR HER,

Sports. One word defines how you shape your life, sports. Sports have always been a part of your life. It is how you found friends, how you learned to play with others, how you learned about success, how you learned about failure, how you learned about pain, how you learned about discipline, how you learned that nothing in life quite gives you that exhilaration of a last-second, game-winning shot (although you can relive that moment in your head forever). You will be doubted, you will be yelled at, you will be looked at to lead, you will be upset, you will compete, you will cry, you will win, you will laugh, you will fail, you will have no idea what you are doing, you will not know how to do all that has been asked of you—but in the end, you will succeed.

Twenty years from now, you will look back on your playing days as some of your favorite memories in life. You will think about all those two-a-days you used to have to do, all the hours of shooting and drills you did, how you spent more time in the gym than anywhere else in life … and secretly wish you had the time and energy to do that all over again. You will think of the sprints you had to do for punishment and, again, secretly wish you could have someone looking over you making you sprint. You will think about how you would play four or five games a day during AAU and wonder how you had the energy to play that much— and then your body will probably hurt just thinking about it. You will think of all the hours you spent in the gym working on improving your game, focusing on more reps, and mastering your craft. It is not until those playing days are over that you will realize that you were doing more than perfecting your shot, you were developing your work ethic for life. Sports is connected to life more than you know.

When your playing days are over, it does not mean your life or your identity is gone, even though it will feel like that for some time. It just means that you will have to use everything you have learned, experienced, and worked for and apply it to succeeding in life. At the time, you did not realize how much fun you were having because you were so focused on not messing up. You were focused on not getting yelled at and worried about making mistakes. Let me tell you something, you are going to make mistakes. You will get yelled at for making mistakes. You will have games where you just are not mentally in the game. That's sports. That's how it goes. The point is to not dwell on a missed shot, a turnover, a bad game. Move on, learn, enjoy the experience. The reality is that if you miss a shot, it does not mean you fail. The only failure is in not trying, not putting in effort, not putting in the reps, not showing up to get better, and not giving your best to your sport. Put in the work, get better, and enjoy the ride. HAVE FUN!!

Here is another spoiler alert: you will also get yelled at, A LOT, by your coaches throughout your career. You don't realize it at the time, but them yelling is more about them than it is about you. It will hurt. It will make you question your ability to play sports, but do not let them get to your head. Getting yelled at for messing up does not define you as a person or even an athlete. Coaches have more of an influence on young kids' lives than they realize, but do not let them get into your head and kill your spirit. Do not let them take the love of the game away from you. You have a short window to play sports, so enjoy it. If you do not have a coach that is cheering for you and wants the best for you (even if they do occasionally yell; I mean, sometimes you will deserve it), find a mentor who can and will push you to be better, that encourages you, helps you to turn your weaknesses into your strengths, pushes you to step outside of your comfort zone, and focus on the positive. Side note: having a mentor will become helpful in life, and not just in sports.

Everything that you learn from sports and playing on a team you will be able to apply to your career and life. You may, and most likely will, one day have a boss who will remind you of one of your coaches, and you will know how to handle the situation. You will remember your playing days and think of the adversity you went through, the struggles you overcame, the teammates who turned into lifelong friends, the hours you spent in the gym working on getting better, and the games you won and how it felt, for that moment, to be on top of the world. Plus, you will have fun stories to tell your coworkers every time March Madness rolls around, which may or may not become more embellished as the years go on. You should have seen my 360 between-the-legs dunk in my last college game—but that story is for another time.

There will be times when you want to quit, but you never do. There will be times when you think you are not strong enough, but you are. There will be times when you cry, both sad tears when you fall short, and tears of joy when you reach your goals (and, again, every year when you watch One Shining Moment at the end of March Madness and any sports movie #sportsheart, but I digress). When you look back at your playing career, you will forget the bad parts, the times you could barely move because you sacrificed your body, the parties you gave up because you wanted to put in more reps in the gym, the lost sleep the night before the game because you were so excited to compete; these are the memories you will take with you. Before they turn into memories, though, embrace the moment.

Love the journey. Enjoy the game. Work hard to get better every day. Enjoy the two-a-days. Embrace the sprints. Have fun playing four to five games a day. Forget about the missed shots, the turnovers, the losses. Love every minute of your playing days because they are short. When it is all over, you will look back and see how much fun you had and be thankful for the memories with your teammates and best friends for life. I'm crying as I write this because of our sports heart.

Your future you,

Deanna Cordova

## DEAR HER,

People will tell you that because of your short stature you cannot be a pro tennis player. "Just face it, you are too small; enjoy tennis recreationally." said a coach. You will carry the memory of your pediatrician telling you after x-raying your hands that "...you will not grow anymore; this will be your height." You will try out for a professional soccer team and will be told you cannot be a goalie because you are too little.

I'm not going to lie to you—being small will be the most challenging hurdle you will overcome in your athletic journey; but guess what, you will overcome it! Your biggest challenge will become your biggest motivator and strength. The words "you cannot" will be replaced by your mantra: "I will, just watch me." Hard work, perseverance, never giving up (there will be times you will want to), working smarter, understanding your body's limitations, getting the right people in your corner, developing a mindset that will allow you to achieve many goals, including playing professional soccer as a goalie; and being part of a National team because you had the right people in your corner. They gave you the courage and strength to achieve the unachievable. As you get older, it does not get any easier, people still judge you by your size. You will continue to challenge society's norm on height and athleticism.

Love,

*Alex Sachs*

# DEAR HER,

Transitions can be hard. The logistical changes that come with a move to a new city or relational changes that come with a new team are challenging. However, I have learned that difficulties can also stem from issues that unknowingly took root long before the actual transition ever takes place. The transition itself just wakes the dormant issues and brings them to the forefront. I considered myself a very confident person during many of my major transitions. Yet, I struggled, because I had allowed people-pleasing to creep in unrecognized and weave itself into the fabric of who I was and what I valued. During times of transition, I found that it was easy to get caught up in how I was viewed and what other people thought of me. In order to navigate life's transitions, establish a set of core values that are important to you and focus on those rather than the ever-changing standards everyone else will set for you.

***Transition 1: Pleasing Boys.*** Have you ever watched a makeover TV show? In my mind, moving from sophomore to junior year of high school felt like what I imagine running through the life-size picture of your old, pre-makeover self would feel like. Of course, my makeover consisted of a "Great Clips" haircut, self-tanner, and hand-me-down clothes from my older sister's closet. Regardless, the change in my appearance garnered more attention from the opposite sex. Without even recognizing it, I slowly began to spend more time and effort trying to impress the boys at my school. My clothes, my words, and my actions all became fixated on the end goal of male praise and attention. In only a few months, I was no longer aware of either the image I was portraying or the one I wanted to portray. I had lost sight of who I was apart from how boys viewed me.

***Transition 2: Controlling Food.*** I entered my freshman year of college with nervous excitement. I had loved my high school experience in the Midwest and was confident with my decision to try out college in Los Angeles. I knew college years were supposed to be some of the best of my life. I felt prepared to build new relationships and challenged by a new role on my basketball team. What I did not foresee was how, when I lost control in areas like friends and basketball, my drive for perfection would lead me to try to take control in more obscure aspects of my life, like the food I put into my body. After feeling so confident and prepared upon entering college, I never would have predicted developing bulimia by the end of the first semester and having to attend mandatory counseling sessions in order to be permitted to play basketball again. I had an extremely unhealthy view of myself and had lost sight of who I was apart from my physical appearance.

***Transition 3: Satisfying Coaches.*** The summer after my freshman year of college, a new coaching staff was hired. After conducting one gym workout, my new head coach encouraged me to transfer because, "You will never set foot on the court." Never one to shy away from a challenge, I knew I could prove him wrong. However, at the time, the weight of knowing the coaches did not want me was overwhelming. Beyond not wanting me, they thought I was a horrible basketball player and unworthy of my scholarship. I vacillated between staying to prove them wrong or leaving to rid myself of the stress. I cared so deeply about being accepted by my coaches and viewed as a talented player in their eyes, that I considered transferring. I had lost sight of who I was apart from my coaches' opinions of me.

It has taken me years to pinpoint why I continued to struggle during times of major transition. I repeatedly lost sight of who I wanted to be because I was looking to please and be approved of by everyone. I did not have a compass to keep me on course. Pleasing boys, controlling food, and satisfying coaches were just three of many ways I pulled away from the person I wanted to be. I cared what my sorority sisters, teammates, siblings, parents, and friends-back-home thought of me as well. While it is important to be aware of how you are presenting yourself to others, it cannot be your true north. I believe you need to be rooted in something greater than yourself to remind you who you should aspire to be and from where your worth comes.

After my senior year of college, my truth north became Jesus Christ. He is all-powerful, all-knowing, all-present, and unchanging. The guidelines He outlines and lessons He teaches have allowed me to navigate the rough waters of transition, rather than be a wave tossed and blown by the wind of other people's opinions. Your worth is not based upon what other kids in your grade think of you, who does or does not ask you to the dance, who you are dating, or what clique you belong to. It is not based upon how much you weigh, what brand clothing you wear, or who your parents are or aren't. Your worth is not based upon if you make the team, how much playing time you get, what your coach thinks of you, or if you miss the game-winning shot. You have value because you are a precious child of a God who loves you, goes before you, will not forsake you, and will not fail you. He is the same yesterday, today, and forever. Don't allow the chatter of other people's opinions to drown out that truth.

If your school offers Young Life, AIA (Athletes in Action), or FCA (Fellowship of Christian Athletes), I encourage you to give it a try and get involved. They can introduce you to a life-giving perspective that will leave you forever changed.

Sincerely,

*Allison (Jaskowiak) Kennedy*

## DEAR HER,

Hello! This is you several years in the future, not necessarily wiser, but let's say more experienced. At your age, I wish I knew the things that I do today, but everyone has to live and learn. The least I can do now, however, is share some of the learning lessons I've acquired through the years.

If I told you the things you've accomplished today, you'd probably laugh, and no lengths of convincing would make you believe it. You've never been anywhere near where you wanted to be. Out of the nineteen short years I've been alive, I can say eighteen of those will be spent being way too hard on yourself. The thing is, you were only making yourself worse. In the world of softball, one year you went zero for twenty-eight at bat and were too timid to walk with confidence when playing shortstop. In the social world, you stayed in a relationship with someone extremely toxic for you for two years, yet never took a stand for yourself. You let those things eat at you, but when you get older, you'll realize it all happened for a reason. You had to learn, you had to figure out yourself, and I thank you for sticking all of that out.

Please do not feel ashamed of yourself. I know you're feeling like a failure. I know you don't want to show up to practice because everyone's signed to D1 schools and you're always the weaker girl who's one step behind. I know you don't want to go to class because people will use you to do their homework. I know you don't want to go to lunch because you will have to see the person you're supposed to be in love with. Here's the thing, straight up. You have nothing to feel ashamed of. The majority of the time, your mind is spent being hard on yourself, and that shouldn't be the case.

Here's something for you to look forward to. Today, you can call yourself an athlete and truly live up to the definition. Today, you reach your own standards. Today, several schools are interested in you, and you know you don't want to go to a D1, because you value your happiness more than image. You've achieved some incredible things. From just your first year of college, you have been named the Player of the Year, Freshman Athlete of the Year, Offensive MVP, and Defensive MVP. Your senior year of high school, you were a CIF champion and received the golden glove award. Those are just some of the titles you've been awarded. I'm not proud of those, though. I'm proud of you for being voted the hardest worker on the team. I'm proud of those accomplishments because they say you're driven, loving, and underneath it all, you've stayed true to yourself. People see those titles.

The truth is, no one will remember these things about you. YOU won't even remember those things about you! You don't even remember you won CIF; that ring just sits and collects dust. No one cares that you won that anymore! Once your team won, you never thought about winning again. Instead, every day you think about wanting to go to lunch one more time with those girls you played with. You never think about the awards you won your first year of college. Every day, your heart breaks a little more, wishing you could play with those girls one more time, wishing you had another hug or laugh with them. Now that I'm a little bit older, I realize the hardest thing in life is knowing great things won't last forever. You won't get to play with those girls forever and you won't have the luxury of living at home and going to college. Hold on to these memories and don't go one second without appreciating them.

I'm proud of you for finishing with a 4.0 in high school and truly wanting to learn in college. You don't care about learning right now; I know you don't. However, learning is the most important thing in life, and you'll meet Professor Abbani soon enough to teach you that. Keep the people who make you passionate for life close to your heart.

I know I'm jumping from topic to topic a lot, but you're such a hypocrite sometimes! Your life advice to people is to remember that life shouldn't be taken so seriously. Life should always be enjoyed, because the people and the fun stories you share with others are the things to live for. Why do you take life so seriously, then? You set yourself up for failure, emotionally and mentally, more times than not! Stay on top of your things, but don't stress as much as you do. KEEP YOUR VALUES STRAIGHT. You know what they are. They're unconditional love, friends and family, working to enjoy life, and creating a purpose in something only you can understand.

I'm proud of you. Don't be so hard on yourself! I love you, so remember to always be you. You owe yourself that much. You deserve to love yourself. Now is always a good time to start.

Love always,

# DEAR HER,

I started swimming competitively at age ten. My mom signed me up for the local swim team because many of the kids in my neighborhood swam on the team and I didn't have many friends. When I started on the team, I *sucked* for the first two summers. I was the slow girl you did NOT want on your relay team. I didn't like being *that girl*, so I decided to change things. In the middle of my second summer on the team, I asked one of the best swimmers, Tim, for private lessons to work on my flip turns, my strokes and my starts and finishes.

Tim pushed me to work harder than I had ever worked before in my 12 years of life. I recall feeling frustrated often, but I didn't quit. Within one summer I began to swim faster, and by the following summer, I was one of the fastest swimmers on the team. I competed and placed in the Arizona State finals every year after that.

Fitting in as a great swimmer switched on the fiercely competitive athlete inside of me. I was afraid of losing the confidence and place on the team that I had gained after being such a slow swimmer. This fierce competitiveness transferred to almost all other areas of my life. If I didn't win a race, I would stomp into the bathroom after the race and cry (quietly) in one of the stalls. I called myself a failure if I lost a race (placing second place or lower), or if I fell short of the picture I had created in my head of who I *should* be to be loved, successful and happy. Somehow, I had come to believe that winning races, getting the best grades and being "perfect" in all areas of my life defined me as successful, happy and even more loveable. It took me many years and several missed opportunities to realize that this was flawed thinking.

If I could go back in time and talk to *me* as a 14-year-old girl, I would share three pieces of advice with "me" that I learned later in my life. Knowing these things earlier in my life would have led to many earlier successes, helped me enjoy the ride more and saved me from my own self-afflicted abuse for being a human.

*Thomas Edison was asked one time, by a reporter, "How did it feel to fail 1,000 times? Edison replied, "I didn't fail 1,000 times. The light bulb was an invention with 1,000 steps."*

# *FAILING IS A NECESSARY PART OF SUCCESS*

I'm pretty confident that we all like winning much better than losing. But I got confused somewhere along the way when I was a teenager. I believed that I was defined by winning or losing. I was a "successful person" if I won and a "failure" if I lost. What I know today is that while we all feel better winning, the only way losing or failing defines anyone, as a failure is if they quit or don't change and learn from each failure.

What I know today is that any type of failure in my life is simply *feedback* that I need to change something in my practice. If you focus on learning from your failures, you will become better each time you try again. If you focus on the failure, and then define yourself as a failure, your performance in sports and life will absolutely get worse eventually. Stay focused on what you want in your life. Learn from every failure, try again and try something different until you get it right.

When you don't give up and you come back from a failure you empower yourself beyond words. This empowerment is something that no person or circumstance can ever take away from you. Feeling empowered is an essential ingredient for your happiness and success and it will make you stronger on the inside, and outside.

## *YOUR SUCCESSES AND HAPPINESS IN LIFE ARE COMPLETELY UP TO YOU.*

Your sport does not define you. Your school does not define you. Your successes and your failures do not define you. Your actions every day define you. Taking responsibility for your life means deciding on and creating a clear vision for the kind of life you want to live and then doing whatever it takes to make that vision happen. You can start defining yourself and your life right now by taking actions every single day that represent the young woman you want to be.

No person, event, or circumstance can crush your vision. You are the only one who holds the power to crush your own dreams and the only way you will crush your dreams is to choose to give up. This is great news, because it means you hold the key to your dreams!

Today I am a business owner, a best-selling author and a leader in my professional industry. There were times in my life that I didn't believe I could ever own a business or become a leader. But I had a vision, and I took action every day no matter what. I've had many failures, but also many successes. I have worked very hard and continue to work hard to achieve my vision for my life. Every failure, every success, every struggle, every win and every loss has helped me get to where I am today. The same is true for you. You get to choose how to interpret your failures and you get to choose to create the life of your dreams.

## *STRENGTH IS AN ATTITUDE*

No human is born strong. Even more, true strength is never just physical. Instead, you decide to become strong by taking actions to create physical and mental strength. Strength starts by making the decision to be willing to step out of your comfort zone to become your best self. Strength is showing up when you don't want to show up. Strength is working harder than you feel like working. Strength is being a good sport when your ego hurts. Strength is pushing through the last set and making it your best set, especially when you're tired and frustrated. Strength is doing the harder thing today because you know it will ultimately make your life better in your future. Strength is learning from failures and trying again even when you are afraid that you'll fail again. Strength is pushing past your comfort zones in all parts of your life to become the young woman you know you are meant to be.

*Strength is an attitude.* It's something you create through your actions every single day. Strength will never just come to you because you wish for it. Physical strength requires mental strength and mental strength requires physical strength. You have all the strength you need inside of you right now to create an extraordinary life, regardless of your circumstances, because you have the opportunity every day to become stronger on the inside.

You have been gifted with this messy, crazy and incredible life and you get to choose to live extraordinarily or to live below your potential. Failure is only a sign that you need to change your strategy and to cultivate your strength by pushing past your comfort zones. The road to success is not glamorous, it's hard work, but it's worth it; I promise! Whether you dig deep to develop your strength, dream big enough and take action every day or not, it is completely up to you.

Don't wait! Start today. I believe in you.

Love,

*Amanda Mittleman*

# DEAR HER,

The mind, heart, and soul are extraordinary and should not ever be underestimated. We live in a fast-paced, media-driven world, and though we can't hide from it, we can control how it affects our time and how we respond to the stressors along our paths. Your mind is much like water; the more turbulent the water, the more difficult it is to see through it. The calmer it is, the more it becomes crystal clear. When life gets too stressful, just remember to take a big step back and BREATHE! Your mind works with your heart, so just breathe and let the love you have in your heart speak to your mind; then you will find your soul—or should I say your soul will find you! When you're in pain, whether physical pain or mental pain, try your best to silence your mind and be still. The soul is phenomenal at healing itself and speaks loudly, as it should, as long as the mind is quiet and calm.

Spiritually speaking, your "heart" refers to your brain and is the place where you feel and do your thinking. Your soul is your "personal spirit," and is the eternal part of your being.

"Spirit" and "soul" are interchangeable, and though you can't see them, they certainly do exist, much like the wind. Your body is a container for your soul or spirit, so use it wisely to express your truth, and respect yourself. Your mind is often referred to as your conscience. Follow your conscience, for it will keep you honest. If you get into a situation where your mind tells you to do one thing, your conscience tells you another, and your gut provides you a with a dominant feeling of which is right from wrong, ALWAYS go with your gut—it won't mislead you!

Should you cross the path of a narcissist, NEVER FORGET, they do NOT possess a conscience mind, and therefore will NEVER own up to the truth or take responsibility for their actions. There are times that the world is EVIL, and though you've done nothing to deserve it, many will attempt—perhaps successfully—to put you to harm. DO NOT LOSE FAITH IN THE POWER WITHIN YOURSELF! You have not failed yourself, though you might think you have, and others might be the first to flash it in your face or on social media. You must learn from your actions, including the not-so-good decisions, the undesirable choices, and ultimately you must "fail forward" to succeed. The most successful people on the planet failed time and time again before they made their fortune or arrived at the top of their mountain. It didn't happen overnight, so embrace the journey, or it's not as fun. What is a narcissist, and why mention it? I'm mentioning this because although you have so much potential to succeed, they will destroy you if you let them. There are haters out there (and a lot them), and they will attempt to rob you of your beauty, mind, heart, and soul, because that's what feeds their empty souls. A narcissist pretends to have values and morals, and they pretend to love and admire everything about you, but inside their mind and behind closed doors, they lie, cheat, insult, steal, disrespect, abuse, criticize, and will never take blame or responsibility for any wrongdoing on their part. They create an imaginary dream world to sweep you off your feet, but once they've got you, it's hard to escape from them, and the abuse begins. Do not let someone toxic control you in any way. Relationships, whether friendships, acquaintances, colleagues, or lovers, should flow in both directions with mutual give and take. If you notice that you're doing a lot more in the relationship to keep things flowing, then take a step back and see if things flow back in your direction. If not, move on without the individual, or it will get worse.

YOU SHOULD NEVER CHANGE YOU FOR THE BENEFIT OF ANOTHER PERSON! Love who you are, and stand firm in what you believe in. Don't chase relationships, whether it's for love, friendship, or for family, because it takes from your self-worth. Just because someone is family by blood, doesn't mean that they are entitled to what you have to give, unless they mutually share respect with and for you. Family can be created by your circle of friends, and in many ways, those can be the strongest of families and relationships! Release all stress and tension from your body and replace that pain with peace. Once your body is calm, then your heart is calm and relaxed. Reevaluate why you are stressed and discover better ways to manage it. Your thoughts many times can create far more stress than what is real. Never stress about things you cannot control! If you have control over things causing stress, just consider your choices and remember every choice has a reward AND a consequence. Sometimes your choice results in an immediate reward, which means the consequence comes later or vice versa, but the point is, decide what your options are for your decisions and choices, and evaluate the pros and cons of each potential result for things of highest priority. No matter how bad your day is going, just remember, it can always be worse! By looking at your day through gratitude, especially in a negative environment, the outcome is typically much more positive, even when things don't go your way.

When all else fails, just smile. It's contagious, and it relaxes the jaw muscle. The greatest revenge for someone who has hurt you or insulted you is a fabulous smile and pure happiness. Those who are mean to others are typically living in their own pain, with self-doubt, and can't stand happiness or the success of others. Every day is a new day, so leave yesterday in the history books, because it's over and nothing can be changed … just learn from it. Don't get caught up looking so far into the future that you miss all the wonderful things right in front of you today. You won't get another chance to experience it exactly as it happens the first time, so make sure to enjoy the little things and celebrate the small stuff. All the wonderful small things that you conquer will lead to much bigger things, and ultimately, "THE DREAM," whatever that may be for you. Live every single day with PURPOSE, PASSION, and LOVE! If you do that, you'll find happiness within yourself … but not as a result from others treating you. Regardless of what you may think, money, power, fame, vanity, prestige, materials—none of them will truly make you happy unless you love yourself first. If you can't find the love within yourself, you need to stop what you're doing and go soul searching until you find it.

You might meet others along your journey who can help you find the love within yourself, but you are the only person who can define what that means to you. Be proud of yourself; there's nothing wrong with that—in fact, it's a personality trait of a super strong woman. Make sure to learn something new every single day. It doesn't take much effort to do that, but it counts when you least expect it. Do not mentally compete or compare yourself to others. There's nothing more distracting and unattractive than a woman who speaks of herself as better or worse than another person. Be better tomorrow than you were today, and be better today than you were yesterday, even if it's only by one percent. Just when you think you're better than you want to be—DO BETTER! You won't ever regret it looking back, and it won't go unnoticed when it counts the most.

"A mistake that makes you humble is far better than an achievement that makes you arrogant." It's so true; be humble, loving, and giving of others when you can. Never give up or sacrifice your dreams or goals for someone else, no matter how much you love them. There's enough room in your life for you to accomplish something you really want, while others are doing the same. It takes coordination, patience, and communication from all individuals in a relationship to achieve personal greatness, goals, and dreams, but it can be done, and the payoff is well worth it. No matter how low life gets at times, always laugh out loud and SMILE! It's good for your mind, heart, and soul. Your current situation is not your final destination, and tomorrow is a day to start over with a blank slate, a new canvas, a new path—a new you! "Maturity is learning to gracefully walk away from situations that threaten your peace of mind, self-respect, values, morals, or self-worth."

Much love,

*Amber Kivett*

## DEAR HER,

I know you're feeling a lot of emotions as you enter your high school years. Here are just a few reminders that I wish I could've known.

TRUST. Whatever you set your mind to, you will accomplish it. Life can take you on different routes, but as long as you focus, you will get there. No matter how short or long. Never underestimate your WILLPOWER to do anything.

LOVE. Practice self-love and love those around you. Don't belittle yourself just because you couldn't do something. Practice, and you'll see that you can get better with hard work. Instead of comparing yourself to others, ask what you can do and learn from them? Stay humble and always practice empathy.

RESPECT. Respect everyone around you, whether it's the janitor, teacher, classmate, or an elder. If you want to be respected, you will have to treat others the same way. It will keep you humble, because everyone has a story to tell, no matter how small or significant their impact may be on you. Apologize when you're wrong and own it.

BE PRESENT. There are moments where you will feel so focused that you forget to be present. Cherish the times you spend with people because there are no rewinds in life. No one will remember what grades you got, but people remember their interactions with you. Cultivate and nurture your relationships but be aware when they do more damage.

LEARN. There is so much to learn in life. Stay hungry to learn because the more you know, the more you can improve. This isn't only for your mental health, but for your wellness emotionally, physically, socially, and spirituality.

If you ever experience bullying, please don't internalize the situation. Sadly, it may be part of life, but you are not the problem; realize that you have family, friends and acquaintances who value you. Don't be afraid to speak and to stand up for yourself or others. Don't entertain negativity.

Trust me, these hard times will pass, and you will experience more to life after high school, so don't miss out on that opportunity!

You will do great things in life, so trust yourself. Be present, love every minute, and respect your journey as you learn in this lifetime.

Love,

*Anna Lynn Dy*

## DEAR HER,

Keep Going. There is no stopping what you can do, what you can achieve, how high you can reach...what YOU are capable of! There may be times where you question yourself, where you stop, where you just can't take it anymore, but let me tell you, keep going. As the great Mahatma Gandhi said, "Joy lies in the fight, in the attempt, in the suffering involved, not in the victory itself." The hard work, the time, the effort, the grind that you put in is all worth it.

I used to let fear stop me from being what I wanted to be, with constant questions in my head, "Will I make the team? What if she's better than me? Am I good enough? Why can't I do it? I have too much to do, what if I can't handle it?" The thing was, the only fear stopping me ... was me. You have to keep going and not let yourself be afraid of stuff that is mere distraction from your goals. Keep going, keep learning, and keep growing!

I learned from my coach to improve on my mental and physical skills. I trained, disciplined, and pushed myself to be the best ME I could be. I became humble, encouraging, and motivating for and from my teammates who always supported me. So, keep going! No fear, no distractions, and no time wasted, you can do this!

:),

*Ashley Nguyen*

## DEAR HER,

For those of you that do not get a college scholarship: This does not mean you are not good enough or that sports did not help develop you to be your best self. Every lesson learned and all growth from athletics will keep pushing you forward. It is your foundation for your education and career that you choose. Cherish those lessons and appreciate all the work that you put into your craft.

For those of you that do get a college scholarship: Congratulations on being the two-percent; that's right, just two percent of high school athletes get a college scholarship. So, when things get tough, just remember that you basically won the lottery!

Your life will be a constant roller coaster of highs, lows, injuries and adjustments; embrace them all. Everything is a learning process, and you are on the best one yet. You will lose games that you gave every last ounce of your effort to. Those games will make you a better athlete and a better person. You will have injuries that will test you mentally and physically; do not obsess about hurrying to get back. Let your body rest and stay sharp mentally. Surround yourself with positivity and teammates and coaches that will build you up while you are sidelined.

When you get to college, just know that all your teammates are at your level or even better, and they all want to be the best. Match them every day. Do not sit back in the off-season and think you have it made, because that is when the other players and your competitors are working the hardest.

Finally, give yourself credit! You have put in countless amounts of hours on your craft and the love of the game. Do not get lost in the hustle and bustle of being a college athlete. Remember your twelve-year-old self that would die if you could not play every day of your life, sitting outside fantasizing about being this star professional athlete. Remember the love of the game because that love is what got you to be the two percent!!!

Love,

Brittney Ducroz

## DEAR HER,

You are taking a new step in your journey, and there are so many things I want to tell you. You are going to experience so much and learn so many lessons, and at times it will feel overwhelming, but you've got this. There will be days where you get up with a fire in your heart, ready to conquer anything and everything that the day has for you. There will be days where you are exhausted (mentally and physically) and you feel like you're pulling yourself out of bed. Those are the days where your focus and discipline will catapult you towards your goals.

There will be days when you feel like you should be accomplishing more. Be careful not to use this feeling to talk down to yourself. There will be days where you see others progress faster than you are. Be careful not to compare yourself, because your journey is not theirs. There will be trials that happen along the way; you will feel heartbreak, there will be health issues with your family, and you will feel like the weight of the world is on your shoulders. Be careful to not let the hurt consume you in trying to process everything at once.

In this moment, the gym will become your therapy. You will truly know what a blessing it is to have this outlet. The gym will give you time to think, to acknowledge what bothers you, and eventually release your troubles. It will give you clarity. It will give you one of the first words you ever identified yourself with, "athlete." You will use this to relate to and help other people. You will learn so many other things on your journey to finding yourself and adding other things to your identity, but you will always be an "athlete."

Love,

Carie Bradshaw

## DEAR HER,

Remember that time that you didn't make varsity softball or field hockey when the rest of your friends did? I know it hurt initially; but let me remind you that you also persevered and became the JV captain for both teams. You were a leader for the girls younger than you and they looked up to you. You set a good example. In field hockey, you continued as an amazing leader as captain your senior year. You should be really proud of yourself for that! I recognize that spring season of softball your senior year was much harder. Despite working your butt off at practice and asking your coaches what you could improve on, game after game you found yourself on the bench. I'm sorry you had to experience that, but I know it made you stronger. I am proud of you for your positive attitude and that you stuck it out. Most of the other girls on your team that were seniors and weren't playing, quit. You were not a quitter. That was something that stayed consistent throughout college, grad school, and now in your career.

Flash forward, your persistence, hard work, confidence, strength, and intelligence have played an integral role in your current success. Yes, there were times that you struggled and times that were hard, but that never stopped you. Just so you know, you have completed a lot of impressive stuff in a short amount of time. By age 23, you received your bachelor's in Exercise Science and a doctorate in Physical Therapy.

Now, after just five years of practicing physical therapy, you have taken on opening up your own physical therapy and coaching business. YOU are a lady boss! All those years of positive attitudes and behavior early on helped lead you to where you are today. There is still plenty for you to learn (but you know that already). Running a business is hard, but you are determined that it will be successful! There will be ups and downs, and that's okay. YOU CAN DO THIS! Never lose that ambitious fire! Now, go show them what you're made of!

Love,

Dr. Danielle Adler Kroot

## DEAR HER,

I am sorry they didn't think you could do gym class or play sports with your friends. It's understandable that you didn't have confidence in your abilities since you were told, "No, you can't" just because of your missing big toe. I think you were stronger than you thought. The "disability" kept you back from ice skating, roller skating, wearing flip flops, and even going barefoot. Gym class was out of the question, and I know you felt like an outsider who didn't belong with your fellow classmates. You made the best of being left out; you made friends with the nurse and you became aware of others who also feel like outsiders. Being told you could not be athletic set you up to believe that you could never be healthy or confident in your body. I know you felt like a failure; your parents were in debt because of all the medical bills.

As an adult, I look back and wish I would have spoken up and tried to be part of the team, even being there to cheer the others on or pushing myself to be more athletic. I see now that I am capable of being active after attending a boot-camp-style class, Monday through Friday. The staff have encouraged me to do things I never thought possible and pushed me to achieve physical and emotional health. I can do almost all the activities, pushing a sled, jumping jacks, burpees, and lifting weights. Two years ago, I successfully competed in a triathlon! I am so proud of you! I feel better than ever about myself and want others to know they can do it, too, regardless of what others say.

Love,

*Dawn Good*

## DEAR HER,

If I had to make one statement about what I've learned in my life, it would be to "be your authentic self." We are all different, no two people are 100 percent alike. The uniqueness that only you have is beautiful and has value in your life. Being your authentic self means self-responsibility for the things that you say or do not say. Actions that are taken or not taken. Creating a foundation of truth, clarity, purpose, and goals that build a strong character should be something of importance to you. Keeping your focus on things that really matter for the long term will just strengthen you; that makes you, you. Be okay with your choices. Sometimes they won't be the best choices but take that adversity and learn from it. The game can be lost, but the learning from the game is always a chance to grow and win.

Being involved in athletics has allowed me to be in touch with my authentic self. I am sometimes goofy, sad, joyous, confused, competitive, wrong choices, great choices—they are all me. Be at peace with who you are. There is no one like you.

I am a competitive weightlifter with American Records in the Snatch, Clean and Jerk, and total weight lifted. I am 66 years old, I will let no one tell me I should not be doing that! Do what you are passionate about. Excellence is the objective. Have no doubt about your success. Continue to move forward, continue taking self-responsibility. Be authentic, for there is no one like you.

Love,

*Deborah Robinson*

## DEAR HER,

Let me start by saying that I am very proud of you and you should be proud of yourself for the choices that you have made. I admire your courage and perseverance during your adolescent years. You were blessed with the talent of being a fast runner, but little did you know that this talent would also come with jealousy, hatred and anger. Being mocked for the color of your skin, not only from non-blacks, the young, the old, but also from those blacks who had a lighter skin complexion than you, with the "good hair." This was a hard pill to swallow. This was unfamiliar territory for you, especially when it came from your own people. What were you supposed to do, how were you supposed to act? There was no manual for this situation, and I know that it took everything in you not to retaliate and respond with the same vitriol as they did, but you rose above that. You stood tall.

I commend you, because at that age you recognized that whatever they said to you was not your issue, it was theirs and you decided to let your feet do the talking. Run as fast as you could, break records, put your stamp on it, because as long as you continued to do that, there was nothing else to be said. Your ability to compete in track & field silenced the naysayers and opened doors for you. From obtaining an athletic scholarship to becoming a national champion and then an Olympian, you created your own narrative.

I am in awe of you, young lady! The choices that you made then, with the guidance and support of those closest to you, have molded me into the woman I am today, and for that I will always be grateful. I'm proud of who I have become and what I have accomplished and that is due to your ability to push through the dark into the light and rewrite the narrative.

I thank you,

Dr. Erica Witter-Davis, DC, DACBSP, CSCS

# DEAR HER,

You have come so far, and I am so proud of you. I remember thinking, wow, I want to be like that girl. I want to stand out, I want to be successful—but what defines success? I used to think it was money and popularity; man, was I wrong. The best type of success comes from within. When you can look at yourself in the mirror and say, "I did it." Your greatest fears, you overcame. That time you wanted to hit for the mile, you did it! YOU pushed yourself to become a better version of yourself. Stop comparing yourself to others or what they have. Material things bring temporary joy, but what happens when your iPhone is no longer the newest one? Are you going to get depressed? No!

Happiness comes from within—you can create it. Stop idolizing celebrities; we don't know their true story. You will hear people tell you, no, don't do that, don't dress that way, you cannot talk like that, but they are wrong; you can, and you will. Remember what brought you to this world; God and your family. Maintain a relationship and respect them both primarily, then you can become happy from within. Protect them, and far more importantly, don't let anyone hurt you or them. Don't be afraid to speak out. Sometimes there is evil out there that wants to bring you down and hurt you, but remember, they cannot break you. You have all the tools to fix it and become better. So, I ask you, instead of getting down on yourself because of something, think, "How can I use this as fuel for myself?" In life there is only one person that can sink you and that is yourself. It is YOU vs. YOU. You have the power to do and become what you want to be! It is not going to be easy, but nothing worth fighting for is easy. You are not always going to be happy, so let it out and cry. Get back up and fight again because we only get one life. Don't wait until it is too late to live your best life.

Love,

Gaby Gomez

## DEAR HER,

You were one of the kids who didn't join a team. I remember. You were afraid, back then, and I remember how severely that fear was felt. You were so used to failure that you were discouraged before you even considered joining a team or trying something new or different. It wasn't considered fun. You would brush off a momentary consideration and justify it by thinking, "I'm not competitive." And yet there were things you did well, that you were encouraged to attempt because you saw someone else involved in it (usually art related) and that, wanting to do as much or more, to some degree was competition. But it had to be on your terms and where you couldn't risk failure. It came from hearing mixed messages, I know; from a lack of emotional support, from being told what you could and couldn't do. Often those messages were in direct opposition to each other, ("You can't get a job, but you will go to college." What's the difference? Both are work.), and as a consequence, you never really felt quite competent or good enough in anything. It came from being criticized at every turn, never being appreciated for what you COULD do or be or accomplish and knowing that in most times and ways you could never be enough. The loser mentality really struck hard with you.

Sports had a huge influence in the area where you grew up. You grew up in a football town at a time when judgments about peoples' activities were very rigid and harsh. If you weren't involved in sports in this town, you were a loser. Football and cheerleading made you a "somebody," but cheering was exclusive. Even girl jocks didn't have the same status as cheerleaders.

Sports would very quickly single out who played hard, who wouldn't, who could, and so you simply didn't try. You knew you would end up at the bottom of the totem pole of worthwhile players before you began. Even more discouraging, if you weren't athletically oriented, the things that WERE possible (being a great writer or artist or dancer) weren't valued as highly. You were not encouraged to follow those paths because you weren't contributing toward something lucrative. Anything outside the prescribed box was looked down on, and that made you feel rebellious, like, "Why would I want to engage in a sport anyway, because I wouldn't want to be a judgmental know-it-all like the 'powers that be,'" and it has colored the way you feel to this day about just about any physical activity that might be helpful or enjoyable (like yoga, hiking, walking, you know—"non-traditional" sports).

Now that I am no longer the little you, I look back and wonder what skills I missed out on developing because of my very rigid, self-imposed, very purposeful avoidance of involvement in physical activity. It had become my expression, and part of my "soapbox" against the unfairness that takes place against people who may not own an inclination toward kinesthetic giftedness.

Where are the holes in my functioning now? Reasonable decision making, quick thinking in a crunch, strategies that support teammates, the consequences of our actions toward the greater good of everyone, or of being a lone-wolf or hot dog or an attention or ball hog? What about the social skills and lessons I missed out on, like learning to lose well—even more importantly, learning to win well without shoving it in someone else's face or dealing well with supposed bragging rights? What about learning the lessons that mistakes and losing are just as important as gaining a sense of healthy self-esteem, or a sense of competence from learning to give it my all, or pitching in to the best of my ability? Or of saving face or preserving my own dignity by having given it the best part of me. Were those lessons I lost for myself by closing that door? I am learning them now, I feel, but more than that, because of this issue alone, this looming sports/

activity/team involvement issue, I see a better you ... me ... the young me ... and the reasons why you couldn't allow yourself to be sacrificed on field for being "the weak link on the team."

Now, because of this, I know better how to be, for myself, what I didn't have back then; support, connection, encouragement for the pitfalls, and to find the gift and the lesson in the victories, as well as in the disappointments. Perhaps this is the important "takeaway" now. I need to remember these ideas when choosing my next yoga class, or tai chi session or finding a meditative path where I can quietly walk in nature. What challenge am I choosing to look at and work on now that younger me ruefully and impulsively disregarded? The whole team concept is one that has come back to me across many situations, where I find I still allow myself to hold back and pay the consequence of being disconnected, or the least motivated, cautiously involved or hesitant. It's not enough anymore to say, "I was bookish and academic," or, "I am an introvert." Am I willing to change the mindset I learned growing up for the challenge of finding a more accepting, braver me, no matter what that may involve? Perhaps that is what is at the heart of this query and my desire to contribute this short piece.

When this desire for a healthier shift in my thinking came about, I had to be ready for what it involved, because

I made a commitment. I made a commitment to myself, my "team," my younger self, the person I have become and the person I intend to grow toward being. This has exposed for me some of the pain that still requires healing, but also reaffirms my new direction. "Allow myself to be challenged." This is the new mantra for me.

Affectionately,

*Gail Doherty*

## DEAR HER,

There will be many times when you doubt yourself, make excuses for why "you can't," fear failure and even experience anxiety over the "what if," but try anyway. These are times when the greatest lessons will be learned. You will find out that you are tougher than you thought, physically as well as mentally, that there are no limits to your capability, and that progress is a success, no matter how small. You will see a new person emerge, someone that does not see obstacles as defeating, but as an opportunity. You will find each day more rewarding, no longer afraid of life, but living with purpose, instead. So, make the effort to show up, put in the work, push boundaries and most importantly, continue moving forward. You have the ability to reach any goal you set for yourself, in your present, in your future, in your life. This is your passion, this is your journey, this is your chance. Push harder for what you want, make the choices that will make you happy, and know that when you look back, it won't be to regret what you have or have not done. Instead, you will reflect on how much you have grown, see the person you were, admire the person you have become, and acknowledge what it took to get here. It will be a beautiful moment, and it will remind you of the strength you have always had. My biggest hope is that you continue to carry it with you wherever you go.

Sending peace and love,

*Genevie Vargas*

## DEAR HER,

For anyone who has ever been doubted by others, or themselves, this is for you. I'm sharing my journey and some of the lessons I've learned along the way because I truly believe that ANYTHING IS POSSIBLE. If there's something you really want in life, go for it!

For me, I had quite the journey with basketball. It was my first love, starting at only four years old, and as time passed, I knew it was my dream to play in college. However, being 5'3" and Japanese-American set some major hurdles along the way. I heard repeatedly from everyone that I was too small, not good enough, and I'd never play Division 1 college basketball. The derogatory comments about my ethnicity were tough as well, but in the end, it only made me stronger and prouder of who I am and where I've come from.

While others didn't believe in me, I didn't care or listen, and I'm happy I had the courage to believe in myself. So, I put my head down and did the only thing I knew how to do;

put in the work. In high school I was the first one to practice, the last one to leave, and would go practice with the boys' varsity team after ours was done. I spent endless hours in the gym working on my game, but unfortunately, when that final buzzer went off, I had zero offers from colleges. I'd be lying if I said my heart didn't ache at the time. However, because I believed so much in myself and knew that success is when preparation meets opportunity, I pressed on. A couple of months later, that opportunity would come, a last-minute exposure camp, where the University of Southern California coaches were there and in need of a point guard. From that one weekend, that was my one and only offer, a full scholarship that truly changed my life.

There were so many lessons I learned in college, but the biggest ones I want to share with you are the following:

1) It will not always be the easiest of roads. Things will happen that are out of your control and you will have to be able to adapt and roll with the punches. After my freshman year we had a coaching change, and with the new coaches, I lost all of my confidence. I started playing afraid to make mistakes and for others instead of myself. If this happens to you, remember why you love this game and why you play. You've never played for anyone else, so make sure you do that and are having FUN. Once I was able to

do that, I played the best basketball of my life and it eventually set me up to play professionally overseas once my career at USC was done.

2) There will always be more talented players that will come, but never give up and always be prepared, because you never know what is going to happen. Heading into my senior year, I was competing for playing time with two of the best point guards in the nation. I knew I wasn't going to receive a lot of playing time, but that summer I decided to work my butt off anyway and contribute the best I could to my team. It's unfortunate, but those two players both suffered season-ending injuries, and I was the only point guard on scholarship and had to play all forty minutes. Thankfully, I was prepared for that moment.

3) And maybe the most important: When all is said and done, no one will remember what your record was, how many points you scored, or how many games you won. But they'll always remember how you made them feel. So be kind to EVERYONE. Teammates, coaches, university staff, janitors, the chefs at the eating halls. These are the people and relationships that will last far longer than your playing career.

These are a few lessons I learned along the way. The last one I'm going to leave you with is that there is no such thing as failure. When one door shuts, another one will open, and although basketball has been the heart and soul of my entire life, it does not define me. It was tough to separate myself from my sport and being an athlete, but like all good things, it will come to an end. And it did. I told myself I would do it until it stops being fun, and when that time comes, choose a career path you're extremely passionate about. For me, that was helping others. There are many different ways I could have pursued that, but I have been fortunate to open my own gym called Torrance Training Lab to improve others' health and fitness. We've built an extremely loving and supportive community, and I look forward to going to "work" every day. Find something you love, and you'll never work a day in your life!

Dream big, work hard, stay humble, and always believe in yourself. Wishing you all the best!

Love,

Jamie Hagiya

## DEAR HER,

LISTEN. I know you are hurting. I know people have disappointed you. I know things may not have been what you believed. You're allowed to feel it all. The good, the bad, the ugly, the sad. And don't you let anyone take that away from you.

FEEL so that you can move through. FEEL so that you can stand taller. FEEL so you can heal.

Feeling does not make you a victim, it makes you human. And the most beautiful thing about humans is our abilities to learn, to grow, and to LOVE.

So, continue loving. Continue giving. Continue caring. The most beautiful thing about you is your ability to see the genuine love, authenticity, and integrity in another human because of the direct reflection within YOU. Hold on to that. It's truly the most beautiful thing about you.

And remember ... Another's actions and behaviors are not a reflection of you. It's a reflection of THEM. No one else can clip your wings. Continue to SOAR.

Love,

Dr. Jen Esquer

## DEAR HER,

This is weird. I'm not really one for profound words or speaking broadly. At any rate, I would like to offer you some small insights I've collected on my own yellow brick road to the City of Oz that we call "Greatness."

What does it mean to be truly great? How do we achieve Greatness? Will we ever arrive there, or is there always more to do? First, I would ask, where do you see Greatness? For me, I know it by the feeling. It's in the places where feats of human courage, perseverance, and talent are displayed. It's in the presence of people who are passionate about creating good in the world. It's sometimes impressive, and sometimes it's inspiration. Greatness is not always on display. Contrary to society's common belief that louder and more flamboyant is better and greater, that's not the case. Sometimes it just is. Sometimes it's the quietest thing in the room. Why do you think so many "great" people are recognized after they're gone? What do you feel in the presence of Greatness? Sometimes I am called to action by it. Sometimes I am inspired or convicted by it. But I am always moved by it, sometimes simply by the sound of a name. Sometimes it's a feeling in the stomach. A stirring and motivation so deep, it threatens to change my biochemistry and drives me to act. The core of Greatness is consistent goodness. It's gratefulness. It's kindness. It's openness and graciousness and generosity. Whether it's loud or quiet or recognized or not, it matters. Some people are impressive and motivational, but the practice of true Greatness is a rarity. It takes courage. Endurance. Authenticity. Truth. It's great to score goals. It's great to break records. But that Greatness will be surpassed by the next person and someday forgotten. It's very nice to have your name listed among others in a book. But did the world change, were people moved, and was society impacted by this alone? Goodness multiplied (or "Good*") is Greatness.

You, dear her, were given a unique package of gifts, ideas, and personality to impact the world for the better. Exercise this in the most honest, open, and kind way that you can. That's being great!

Do not sell your soul for success or reputation or money. I promise that, whatever the situation is and however promising it seems, sacrificing your values for socially acceptable or speedy fame will never be worth it. It only makes you resentful at the end, even if you get the money and recognition you wanted. Sometimes leaving is the best thing you can do, and you are capable of doing that.

Learn to be patient. Learn how to work hard. This will always win over talent that does neither. Run the marathon. Play the long game. You'll find a lot of competition in miles 1-7, or the first half, but there are very few still hanging on in the last quarter.

Get to know yourself well, and as soon as possible. Self-improvement and personal development will never be a waste of time. Take the time to regularly invest in it. Make you better, so that you can give and serve and teach and play better. A lot of people are going to tell you about yourself. They will try to tell you who you are from how they see you. Don't take that too close to your heart; only you know who you are. You have walked a unique path and have unique things to offer. Let other people's words guide you; treat those words as the feedback that it is but remember that it isn't gospel truth. Only you truly know you. Start early.

You are not supposed to know everything. Ever! It's okay to look back on your life, even on last year, and wonder, "What was I thinking?" It means you're growing, and you know better now. Never stop learning. Get a mentor. You're not supposed to be an expert, but you can find someone who is. Look for someone who does or has done what you dream of doing, beg them to teach you everything they know, and then pass that on to someone else, too. And don't forget to give them value back. Find people who value the same things you do, whether you walk similar paths to Greatness or not. I can honestly tell you that doing this alone will be impossible. It will make you lonely, tired, and, maybe, sick. Nobody is truly self-made; ask for help when you need it and find people to walk with you. If you're alive, there is still something for you to learn. But, also, you don't have to learn every second of every day. Do your best work with maximum focus, and then take a break, already.

You are drawn to things for a reason. Pay attention to them, meditate on them, connect with them. They will help to guide you in your life and your purpose. They aren't an accident. When you have no idea what you are doing, think about why you started and what moves you. That will get you back in line again.

You are going to be okay. Good luck on your journey on the yellow brick road. That is where Greatness is; it's not an end destination. Do not strive for it. Be it in the kindest, most open, most you way possible.

To your greatness,

# DEAR HER,

First things first, have no regrets; everything that goes on in life is either a blessing or a lesson. It all happens for a reason and some things aren't fully controllable; for the tasks that can be controlled, complete them to the best of your ability regardless of the backlash you may receive. With that being said, I wish you the best on your journey. Here's some advice I wish I was given early on as a student-athlete …

## High School

Work to achieve your goals in the classroom and on the court. Write down goals for both academics and basketball, set high standards for yourself and be able to hold yourself accountable. You can do this by having your goals and standards placed on your bedroom wall or anywhere visible, written down, so you will be able to refer back to it every once in a while. It's great to constantly have that reminder of what the big picture is. High school is a time where a lot of kids fall into peer pressure and go on to be the follower with the wrong group of people. Don't feel the need to change for anyone, especially if it's not going to help you attain your goals in life. Be yourself and refer back to those standards.

By now you should know whether you're in the group of people who like school or if you're just doing it to get by and stay eligible for your sport. I would advise you to push yourself in the classroom during your four years of high school. I surely wish I had. I earned all A's until junior year, when I received my first B grade. I needed more of a challenge academically and it was recommended that I enroll in AP, but I didn't want the challenge to overshadow basketball. I wish I would've at least given it a chance. My advice to you would be to listen to your school counselors and the advice they give about college, in addition to research on your own, if needed. If you can take AP classes and pass them, it will be a huge help when you make it to college. It could possibly allow you to graduate earlier, in three to three-and-a-half years rather than the normal four-year route. This could perhaps result in your graduate school being paid for. With that being said, the easy way in high school will become the longer way in college.

## The Recruiting Process/Keep Options Open

If you put in the kind of quality work you need to as a basketball player, college letters of interest will begin to come.

When they do, know that they are not offers but just simply interest, that coaches notice you and you are on their recruiting radar. Many other players may be receiving these same letters, so don't get cocky and comfortable in the position you are in. Keep working on and off the court to achieve the goals you've listed.

If the colleges aren't knocking at your door and you've reached your junior year, it is okay to try to contact them in order to get attention. Get help from a coach; it's okay to send out film and reach out to them. Know that just because they didn't find you doesn't mean they don't want you. Colleges go out to look for players at viewing tournaments, practices and league games. Some of these events you may not happen to attend, or you could be overlooked. Many of the coaches end up trying to get the same ESPN Top 100 recruits, and you if aren't a part of that group, then who do you think they'll come to when those players don't choose their school? It could be you. Don't allow your pride to get in the way. A scholarship is a scholarship and many girls wish they had the opportunity to even consider getting their college tuition paid for in exchange for doing something they love.

Within the recruiting process, I can't stress enough that questions need to be asked. Ask the coaches what they saw in you as a player, what you can work on prior to arriving if you choose their school. Ask about other recruits/commits so you'll know who you'll be with and take notes on all these answers to better yourself. On the academic side, check to see if the school offers majors you're interested in, and also if the coaches make athletes alter their decisions for majors if it's a non-favorable concentration with basketball accommodations. For example, some coaches don't allow players to choose certain majors that are known for their difficulty because it could put your basketball eligibility in jeopardy. Honestly, sometimes it's almost like you become an athlete-student, rather than a student-athlete.

Keep your options open regarding your college choice. It's okay to go away from home for an opportunity of a lifetime. Family and friends will always be a phone call away. A mistake I may have made is not considering any colleges out of state. I was so afraid to be too far from home, but in reality, the school I chose had a seven-hour drive from home and ended up being just as far as many of the neighboring out-of-state schools that I didn't consider due to location. With my move and transition from Long Beach to Sacramento, it felt like I was in a completely different state anyway. In the end, I would advise you to make the choice you're most comfortable with, because no matter how close or far away you are, your family and friends won't be there every day living the life of a college student-athlete.

## Burnout/ Escape Route

Burnout is a disturbance I experienced throughout basketball, starting in my high school career just a bit, but heavily throughout college. It was an annoyance, physical and emotional exhaustion with something I originally loved to do. I started to develop a love/hate relationship with the game of basketball, because I was putting in numerous amounts of work and not getting the results I wanted. I had overworked myself to the point of almost endless frustration on the court. It was due to not knowing when to sit back, relax and take a break.

My advice would be to find an escape when things in basketball aren't going the way you planned. If your shot isn't falling, then, yes, you may need to go get shots up, but don't let that task consume your day. Find a hobby, because some days, playing your sport may be the last thing you want to do. In addition, use your resources when you're struggling. Ask teammates with more experience for advice. Find a way to vent your frustrations, don't let them build up to where you're ticking like a bomb and then boom, you explode. Find an emergency escape route or safe zone, perhaps another physical activity, writing in a journal, going to church, sleeping it off temporarily, or using counseling or mentoring services. I didn't use counseling services to vent until my senior year in college. It helped me get over a rough patch just by simply having someone to vent to outside of my daily circle. I was able to overcome all of adversity in my life and eventually returned with a new and more positive outlook on situations. Sometimes you just need to get thoughts off your chest and let them go.

## In the End

Overall, being a student-athlete is a valuable experience that exposes you to many life lessons. It may not be the easiest process, but in my opinion, it's definitely worthwhile. For the time being, enjoy it, know that the bad won't last forever; not having a direct path to success is just a part of life. Be you, keep your eyes on the prize, keep an open mind about life-changing decisions, and don't exhaust yourself into burnout. At the end of your career as a student-athlete, you will look back and laugh at the good times and bad times and they will forever be memories. I wish you the best through your journey.

Sincerely,

Justyce Dawson

## DEAR HER,

"What messes us up most in life is the image in our head of how it's supposed to be."

You often think, "I wish I were more pretty." Be patient. The glasses and braces will be gone by the time you're 16. You will gain and lose a little weight over the years, but always have an average physique. More importantly, you will be very healthy with the exception of a few minor setbacks from which you'll recover, making you even more grateful that you're free of chronic problems. Don't pay attention to TV stars and *Glamour* models; they are the products of round-the-clock trainers and personal chefs, make-up and plastic surgery, airbrushes and Photoshop. While some people spend a lot of time and money obsessing over the latest fashion and the newest gray hair, your life will have much more meaning and happiness than one who spends each day concerned about her looks. You will be judged as a lovely person because of your sense of humor and compassionate heart. You will be regarded as clean and professional in your appearance at work, and you'll be able to relax in a t-shirt and shorts with no makeup at home on a Saturday afternoon. Who needs the stress of always trying to look perfect?

You spend many frustrated moments thinking, "I wish my parents weren't so strict and I wish my brother would quit teasing me." Because of your naiveté, you don't realize that those are indeed expressions of love. Sometime after high school, your mother will tell you how concerned Tom was when you started showing an interest in boys. He will protect you from his acquaintances who are "dogs" and he will invite you to one of his college parties. You and Tom will become great fans of each other, celebrating your milestones and victories. As adults there will be long periods of time that you don't see each other, but when you do, you will enjoy each other's company as if no time had passed at all. And Mom and Dad are strict because you have an adventurous streak that scares them a little. When you finish college, they will turn that fear into admiration, but for now you're still their little girl. They want you to grow up to be respectful of others as well as yourself. They are instilling in you now the discipline and self-control that every person needs; if you don't achieve it early, you might end up getting in an accident, arrested, pregnant, or without a degree. When a parent, teacher or coach gives you a hard time, it means they care. Beware what you wish for. If they leave you alone, it means they've stopped caring.

Despite being part of a happy, healthy family, and even though you have good friends, you sometimes feel like a lonely loser. You are angry a lot of the time for no apparent reason. You will find out later that most of these mixed-up feelings are related to the coming on of puberty, that most 12-year-olds are a little obnoxious. In just a few years, you will be grateful that Mom and Sister Mary Olga (whom you call Old Goat) were as patient with you as they were! It's strange that the process of figuring out who you are can be so painful; no one particularly enjoys coming to terms with their own flaws and shortcomings. But very soon a lot of it will be joyful. You will try new activities like drama and drill team and have loads of fun, even though neither one of those will become your true passion. You will have boyfriends and heart breaks, great classes/teachers and lousy ones, wonderful adventures and periods of boredom. Always choose happiness, because misery is an incredible waste of time and energy. It will all work out for a life that is perfect for YOU.

"You never know how strong you can be until being strong is the only choice you have."

Love,

*Karen Jardine*

## DEAR HER,

I know it is difficult to learn lessons through listening, but today I am going to ask you to try. You will spend a lot of time in this life learning lessons through trial and error, and that is fine. That is how we grow, after all. However, there is some foundational stuff that you need to know before you begin.

1. Remove the pressure to define yourself for other people. I remember being your age and constantly feeling the need to know who I was and act accordingly. Listen to me—it is important that you know that you are not required to please your peers. Popularity and social status might feel like it's the world now, but trust me, it is not. I've been both a band kid, a track athlete, and a cheerleader. The only thing you ever need to be is okay with yourself. Period.

2. Use the same social acceptance and grace for others as you do for yourself. Be accepting and kind always, to yourself and to others.

3.  Don't give up on something you think about all the time. I don't care if you show up every single day and still don't take home the trophy. A life of passion is the greatest trophy. If you spend your days working on things that you feel passionate about, NOBODY can ever take that away. Pursue the things that set your heart on fire.

4.  Remember today and always that you are strong, smart, capable and worthy. This is not a status to be claimed. This is simply just who you are. There will be days you don't feel so strong, smart, capable, OR worthy. But I promise you that who you are is not always how you feel. So, no matter the season or the scenario, remember this and repeat it out loud to yourself often; "I am strong, smart, capable, and worthy."

Love you,

*Katie Summers*

# DEAR HER,

The world will tell you how to be. To be quieter, to be less confident, to not be too loud or too soft; to follow the path that society chooses for you. We are all told as children that we have our own place and our own function in society, but we are never encouraged to figure out where we truly belong. Instead, we are pushed to fulfill dreams that don't always align with what we want for ourselves. We are pushed to ignore the people we want to become in the effort to become a person everyone thinks we should be.

**When your confidence is low:** We tend to let the opinions of others rule our own feelings, even in the things we know we excel at. And at times our confidence dwindles, because we fear judgment from those around us. Confidence comes from within, and we should remember that the only person we need to compare ourselves to and the only person we should really look to impress is ourselves. When we learn to focus our confidence on self-development versus the approval of others, we learn to trust ourselves in what we can achieve.

**When your body image is negative:** As women, we face pressures every day concerning our looks and aesthetics. Take pride in your beauty, because it is not just skin deep. Your body image is more than just the clothes on your back and the belt around your waist, but it is not something that defines you and it is not something that determines your value. The people you see on TV, in magazines, on your Instagram and social media; what you see is not always what you get, and images in the media should always be taken with a grain of salt. Models, social media stars, actors ... they all have bad days and they are all people, just like you. Remember that you are worth more than your body, and that that pimple on picture day will not determine the rest of your life. Eat good food. Eat enough. Exercise when you can. Have fun. Get some fresh air. Love your body, not just as a physical thing.

**When your mindset isn't focused:** Your mindset can be your best friend or your worst enemy, and it's important to recognize when our minds are not in the right places. Sometimes life pulls you in all kinds of directions. Maybe you just can't catch a break. Our focus becomes cloudy, and in the mess of it all, we forget why we do the things we do. We forget who we are and what we want to achieve. It's easy to get lost in the static, but if you stay true to your convictions, true to the things you are passionate about, and you stay honest about what is influencing the way you think, you can conquer all distractions.

**When your work ethic is suffering:** A lot of things can affect your work ethic: relationships, stress, mental and emotional health. And there will be times when you are 100 percent, and times when 10 percent is too much to give. A good work ethic comes from knowing you need to have balance. You need to balance your time and learn to prioritize yourself and your commitments, or else everything you've committed yourself to falls apart. When your work ethic begins to suffer, dial back and look at the bigger picture. Is giving my 100 percent to everything taking away from what I give to myself? Am I spread too thin? Am I not challenging myself enough? What can I do to make what I am doing more enjoyable? Is this commitment sustainable for myself and for others?

**When relationships fall apart:** We are not promised infinity friendships and lifelong connections. Sometimes the relationships you thought would last a lifetime are the first ones to fizzle at the sign of trouble. When relationships fall apart, it may seem like the end of the world, but you have to put a scope on your relationships to see the bigger picture. While one person may decide that their relationship with you wasn't worth the time, know that there is a whole world out there of people looking for the same things you are. There are those in the world that laugh at the same jokes you do, eat the same foods, even have the same shirt you do. The end of one relationship or friendship does not mean the end to all. Sometimes a door has to shut for another one to be opened, and you'll never know who is on the other side. Take chances; step out of your social zone and meet as many people as you can. You never know who will be there to stick around in the end. Why limit your possibilities?

**When you feel alone:** Many people don't like to admit when they feel lonely. But many people don't consider the idea that it is OKAY to be alone and to feel alone sometimes. It is a part of life, and while relationships are important in maintaining a happy one, know and be okay with being alone and having to do things alone sometimes. It can be hard to reach out to someone, especially if you feel like you don't have many people to look to when things are lonely. While it's good to build the courage to reach out for help or to socialize with others, we often forget our own dialogue about our feelings. Learning to be okay with being alone can help you figure out just how self-sufficient and amazing you are. You may even figure out who you are by being by yourself. Learn to step over your boundaries and learn to be comfortable and enjoy being alone.

**When you succeed:** Take joy in successes. Be humble in your triumphs. Never forget the value of your hard work. Spread the wealth of your successes and good things will come from the people you help. Use your successes to create an even clearer path to your future.

To the young athlete reading this today.

To the young woman looking for guidance.

To the lost teenager, yearning for a purpose.

To the fire in you that needs kindling.

To the little girl in my past, that never thought she would amount to anything:

You are special. You will find your way. You will change the world, whether it's your world or everyone else's.

Love,

*Kayla Buenaventura*

## DEAR HER,

Life is never what you expect. Although you have some ideas of what your life is going to be, if there is one thing I've learned over time, it's that you will be met with things you could never have predicted. Being able to make adjustments, accept what you cannot change, and overcome challenges that you never expected are all things that will make your life full.

At your age, I had a life plan. I was going to go to college, start a career and get married. Eventually I wanted to have kids and become a mom. In my mind, life was just going to keep getting better and better as I succeeded in my career and raised my family. I thought life was about continual improvement, opportunity and happiness.

What I didn't know then was that life isn't just about constant improvement or taking advantage of opportunities. Rather, it is about living through all the ups and downs. It is about learning how to weather the storms and appreciate the successes. Life is full of both ups and downs, and success will happen when you figure out how to maneuver through the shifts and changes that occur. Of course, it is also about the people you connect with along the way.

You might understand this if I use the analogy of your sport. When you prepare for a game, you have a plan. You know the basic idea of what you want to happen on the field or on the court, and you have a strategy to win. Then the game begins, and it doesn't quite go the way you imagined. People get injured. The other team uses a different technique. The ball doesn't go where you want it to go. All kinds of shifts happen that you could never have predicted.

If you want to win the game, you have to learn how to handle those unexpected challenges. You can't quit. You shift, adjust, and maneuver in ways you could not have foreseen at the start, and you rely on your teammates to work with you along the way. The people in the game make all the difference!

What's amazing, though, is that if you DO adjust, and if you DO meet the challenges, you will win the game. You will have a lot of fun along the way. My message for you, DEAR HER, is to have a plan for your life, and be aware that the unexpected is going to happen. Learn to handle change. Continue to grow when things don't go quite the way you planned. Build a team of people around you to help you along the way. And be sure you have some fun!

Life is a wave. Enjoy the ups and the downs, and in the end, you will win the game!

With love and best wishes,

## DEAR HER,

To begin, I want to tell you everything will be okay, although I know it may not always feel that way. It is normal to feel this way, but do not stay there long as it is wasted energy. The world needs you! You have the world ahead of you and in the palm of your hand. You can be and do amazing things if you give yourself a chance. Be kind to yourself.

You are likely competitive in some regard, but do not beat yourself down. You undoubtedly have weaknesses; however, do not forget to smile upon your strengths. Love yourself, give yourself permission to be imperfect while working hard to learn and grow. Develop the desire to be a life-long learner. This does not always mean a formal class! Learn about what is around you. Learning about yourself should keep you busy for quite some time, perhaps a life-time. Never stop doing it.

**Life.** You likely do not know where life is taking you, which is just fine. Don't let the pressure to choose a college or a career path get to you. Take the opportunities given to you. They may not lead you to where you will land in your adult life, but these times will help to eliminate what you do not want to do. Don't forget that this is equally valuable, although it may not feel like it in the moment. Knowing where you do not want to be gets you closer to the path you are looking for.

**Faith.** Believe in something bigger than you. Life will not always make sense, but know that there is no mistake in where you are. You can turn your experience into something meaningful to the world. Always believe and have faith.

**Moments.** Moments are not a lifetime. High school is a moment in your life. It feels like your whole world, but really it is a training ground for life. Take healthy risks. No one will remember, care or know that you lost the student government election, the essay contest or that your invitation to homecoming was declined by your crush. Take healthy risks and fail. Feel the pain of failure as this is the fire that makes you into iron when it matters; when you need to make tough decisions and endure adversity. Ask yourself what you can do better and move forward. Baseball players are considered fantastic if they get on base four out of ten at-bats. Basketball players are awesome if they can make three out of ten shots from the field. These athletes will never get a base hit or make a 20-foot jumper if they do not suit up and play. Life outside of sports is no different. Live this way. Suit up and play, but don't pursue perfection. Perfection is an exhausting and unrealistic goal.

**Sports.** In addition to your chosen sport, take kickboxing or jiu-jitsu. Learn how to throw a punch and how to take one. Learn how to fight on the ground. This is life. Just like these sports, life can be ugly and painful, yet masterful and glorious at the same time. Do not wonder if you are strong enough, know that you are. You do not need to master these sports beyond knowing that you have the drive and will continue to fight. It will take time to get to this point but do get there. I would not be where I am now without the discipline of sport and the metaphoric training of martial arts.

**Beauty.** Be beautiful. Not sexy, not provocative, but beautiful. I know this is what you are told by TV, movies, music, billboards, and probably by some of your peers. I can tell you it is a lie! This is a fantasy world. Reality demands that you dress and conduct yourself so that everyone knows you are beautiful, confident and love yourself. You are a force to be reckoned with, not a body to be conquered. However, beauty is not only about you. Never forget the beauty of the world. The flowers, the sunsets and the full moons are all reminders of the vast beauty we live in if we stop to enjoy them. Be beautiful and enjoy something beautiful every day.

**Relationships.** It's okay to be alone. Do not spend time with girls that make you feel "less than" because you are afraid of being alone. Do not go through partner after partner because you do not want to be alone. Be comfortable being alone when the company available does not feed your soul. Feeding your soul is a big task, but if you remain open and friendly, your people will find you eventually. Believe me, it is worth the wait. Also, acknowledge and maintain the happy and healthy relationships you have. These are what will give you strength to do amazing things.

**Give.** There is a great big world around you that needs you. Be observant to those around you. Hold a door, flash a smile, write a note or share your lunch. There is something you can do every day. Small acts of kindness can change the world. It is easy to be a bystander. Being a bystander is weakness. Stopping to record, mock or not help the individual in peril are the dark places of this world. Bring your own light every day. I need you as I age, and your children need you. You are building the future.

Faithfully,

## DEAR HER,

As you embark on the exciting journey of high school sport, you will undoubtedly face challenges. All athletes are susceptible to challenges such as injury and harsh criticism for underperforming, but female athletes have a special set of circumstances which makes the challenges we overcome our superwoman power!

Unfortunately, there are still people in the world who look to women's sports as second class or mediocre. If you ever hear this garbage, speak up and speak out! Know that what you do is daring and courageous. You are highly skilled and highly trained and only a small segment of the population has achieved what you have been able to achieve thus far. You have so much more to do! Remember this.

No matter what sport you play, where you play or how often you play, injury is likely to make its way around the block a time or two. Unlike our male counterparts, we tend to recover and bounce back quickly. But that doesn't come without struggle and the onset of fear. It's important to have a short-term memory in sports; allowing a negative thought to linger causes stress, which leads to non-performance. Heal, recover and leave the injury in the past. The human body is amazing!

Do we even need to discuss the changes we go through on a monthly basis? No. However, I will say that adapting and overcoming the physical demands of sport during our least favorite time is truly our superwoman power! We also need to pay attention to our ever-changing hormones and emotions when dealing with our peers, teammates and coaches. It's important to find what works for you to curb pain and make you the most comfortable. Prepare for these times.

In my experience, the best part about team sports is the lifetime of sisterhood bonded by experience. In your most challenging times, look to your right, look to your left. Never underestimate the power of teamwork, the power of hard work and determination.

I began playing team basketball in 9th grade. Yes, I was a late bloomer. At 6 foot, 2 inches, I was faced with the challenge of matching what others perceived my skill level should be, with what my actual skill level was. My family, coaches and teammates saw the potential in me and wanted me to succeed. I realized then that I was in the small segment of population with this opportunity, but I had to play catch-up, and fast. I practiced hard and knew that I had four short years to make something happen for myself. I thank God, He blessed me with true talent and athletic ability. I'd become a young superwoman!

By my senior year in high school, I'd been heavily recruited by top programs around the country. I thank God I earned a full-ride scholarship to college! I was excited and terrified. I wondered if I really had what it took to play Division 1 basketball at the premier level. Could I live up to the expectation of my current coaches, future coaches, family, and friends? The answer was yes. With the help of my coaching staff, which included my strength and conditioning coach, Leslie Trujillo (Coach C), my confidence shot through the roof and I continued to break out of my basketball shell.

After college, I went on to play professionally overseas in Burgos, Spain and China. As I reflect on my high school and college basketball journey, I know that my success came from the challenges I overcame along the way. Challenges come and go, but on this journey, you will not be alone!

Love,

## DEAR HER,

Remember to treat your body well. As an athlete, your body will frequently be on display for others to critique. You will have critics, but also remember that you will also have people who are your champions—when you are struggling with your weight, when you are struggling to nourish your body, let those voices be the voices who ring truest and cheer the loudest. Your body will take you far. It will get you through high school and club, through four years of being a D-I student-athlete, through weights and conditioning, stress fractures and cortisone shots. You'll learn how to fuel your body, you'll learn to be kind to your body, and one day you'll even learn to love your body.

Remember that sometimes school may not be easy, but sports will be your equalizer and the challenges your academics will put before you are only fostering the grit and resilience it will take to compete at the level you one day will achieve. And one day, to your surprise, you'll be named three years in a row to the Big West All-Academic Team.

When life gets tough, volleyball will be there. When life gets tough, your teammates will be there. When life gets tough, your coaches will be there. When life gets tough, your family will be there.

Remember, sports are going to allow you to connect with other girls in a way you never thought possible. The literal blood, sweat, and tears will bond you. When you meet these girls, hold onto them tight. They are the ones who will lift you when you are down. Allow yourself to lead them and allow yourself to be led. Leaders don't always lead from the front—remember this.

Remember to allow yourself to be amazing, allow yourself to be inspired, and allow yourself to believe that you will one day inspire others.

Love,

Lindsay Drennen

## DEAR HER,

It's okay to be done; everyone will be some day. Whether it's the end of high school, college, or your pro career, it's okay to remove "athlete" from your resume. It's a part of who you are, not your entire description of worth. In the years to come, you will suffer the devastation of loss and you will feel an indescribable abundance of joy, neither of which will have anything to do with a scoreboard in an arena. However, never underestimate how ingrained that word is on your heart. You will experience so much life in the years after you stop calling yourself an athlete, but that word will forever live in your soul and it shapes your life in ways you cannot see yet.

Right now, it feels like you're pouring everything you've got into being an athlete: your time, your social life, your body, your sanity. Most days it's a struggle, because you want perfection, you want that ever-elusive praise from your coach. Some days, it feels harder than it is worth. But it is worth it. Being an athlete is building you and the woman you will become.

After four years away from the game, you will come back to it with a renewed enthusiasm and from a completely different angle. You will go from player to mentor and coach. You will guide other girls through their formative years, and you will be able to do this knowing that while they endlessly strive for perfection like you did, the "perfect" days aren't the days that make them better.

Your body will always ache from injuries sustained and your weight will fluctuate, but your physical strength and your confidence will not waiver. You will ask your body to do the seemingly impossible: carry and deliver a child, and then get back into the shape it was. Your body is the body of an athlete and it will do as you ask.

The girls who fight beside you on the court will be the girls by your side at your wedding, the girls who will like every stupid baby photo you post on social media, the girls you will text when your dad dies. Just like sisters, it doesn't matter if you talk every day or once a month, they're still there, and, when you're together, it's the same even when everything else is different.

At times, it does feel as if the word "athlete" is stealing everything from you, but please know, it's the exact opposite; it's giving you all the tools you need to build a life. So, it's okay to be done when that day comes, because regardless of whether you ever touch a ball again or not, your insides are the shape of an athlete. And that means you don't quit.

In Love & Strength,

*Lissa Booth*

## DEAR HER,

You will be underestimated in all aspects of your life. It will at times be so subtle that you may not even notice it till later, and at times it will be so blatant you'll have to do a double-take.

It will hurt your feelings. It will feel like the wind got knocked out of you. It will make you question your decisions and your goals. It will make you feel less than whole. It will hang over you like a rain cloud moving in on a sunny day. It will stick with you like super glue.

You will pretend it didn't happen. You will laugh it off. You will play the scenario repeatedly in your head. You will believe them. You will internalize it. You will hide. You will quit. You will cry. You will scream. You will try to figure out what is wrong with you. You will underestimate yourself. You will get up. You will brush yourself off. You will adjust your plan. You will rise to the challenge. You will prove them wrong.

It's not always going to be easy. Sometimes, you'll work twice as hard and it won't be enough—BUT that doesn't mean that you aren't enough. Your opinion of yourself is what matters in the end. It will take a while, decades even, but you will come to know your worth, your worth to yourself and the communities you inhabit. You will learn who you are, and it will inform who you want to be. Once you start on that journey forward to self-worth and truly begin believing in yourself—watch out world! I use the words "journey" and "forward" deliberately, because there is no end point, there is no time limit, and you will never go back to where you started from. It's going to be scary and it's going to be hard, but it's liberating at the same time. Trust yourself.

The best part of the journey you are going on is that you won't have to do this on your own. You already know people and will come across more throughout your life who are in your corner, helping to push you and support you through the journey. Trust your tribe. You can't do this alone. I know it's hard to ask for help but asking for help does not make you a failure. But don't worry, there will be a bunch of really great ones that you don't even have to say anything to, they will just be there when you need them. You will be underestimated, but you will be amazing.

Much Love,

Maureen James

# DEAR HER,

It's been a minute since I hung up my jersey for the last time at Gersten Pavilion. I was a student-athlete at Loyola Marymount University for five years (red-shirted my second year due to injury) competing at the highest level that many athletes, including myself, manage to climb to—NCAA Division 1 Volleyball. At the end of my sophomore year, headed into junior year of high school, I signed my National Letter of Intent to play at LMU.

I graduated from high school a skinny, hopeful string bean, and packed my bags for summer training with the LMU strength and conditioning coach. Over the course of the next five years, I had no choice but to transform from a skinny and hopeful me to a much more physically- and mentally-stronger version of me. I remember going through 2-3 shirts per practice (had to change so the floor wouldn't get slippery from sweat); lifting heavier weights than some of the male athletes (volleyball players have strong legs, y'all); and being forced to take ice baths before being allowed to leave the training room (because soreness is really real after three-plus hours of practice and an hour of strength & conditioning).

If you would've told me then that I'd miss those things six to seven years later, I would've laughed in your face (or slapped you upside the head). But here I am. I may not miss those particular things, per se, but I miss the feeling—the feeling of being so physically, mentally and emotionally challenged and drained at the end of the day and waking up and doing it again the next day, because that's what we do. That's what athletes do. That's what teammates do. You don't let your team down; you have no choice. I'm still an athlete at heart—you never lose that—but I no longer have a team pushing me and holding me accountable. No one will be directly affected by my choices. No one will know if I go through the motions at a workout, don't finish my reps or flat out don't show up to the gym. No one will make me run or bench me or yell at me. No one will see me fail.

It's taken me a number of years to fully understand why that mentality is wrong. I have myself to push me and hold me accountable. I will be directly affected by my choices. I will know if I don't show up. I will see me fail. And I matter. You matter. Your opinion of yourself is the one that matters the most, come to find out. The body can withstand almost anything; I proved that to be true for myself in college, and many people, including you, prove that to be true in extraordinary ways every single day. It's the mind that needs to be convinced. It's the mind that needs to be trained. It's the mind that needs to be made up—not for anyone else's benefit but our own. That's my challenge for you, strong, powerful girl. To love yourself so much that you show up to practice, you give it your all, you push through even when you don't think you can do it, because years later, I promise you it will pay off in ways you can't begin to imagine now.

Sport is not just sport. It's much bigger than that.

All my love,

*Megan Nash*

## DEAR HER,

You are a game-changer. Have courage and be kind. Display your courage by the way you carry yourself in difficult seasons of life. Display your courage by confidently attacking issues that nobody else will.

Remember, you are important. What you believe in is important. You have the ability and responsibility to create change and to start a movement.

You never know how hard life is for the girl you are facing in competition. Someone you compete against may be battling the deepest, harshest reality of depression or high anxiety and she has found sports as an outlet and escape from the pain. Major life events in family or in friendship circles may be affecting her.

Maybe, just maybe, at the end of the game, you are the first person that day who looked her straight into her eyes, shook her hand, and sincerely thanked her for the competition and complimented her on her performance. You never know.

Have the courage to stand out in the crowd, not in a flashy look-at-me kind of way, but in a way that helps recognize the presence of other human beings around you. Recognize the good in the people around you, because you might be the only one who makes them feel like they matter.

You have the opportunity and the responsibility to shine your light and give hope through the way you courageously attack each day. May the courage you display create a ripple across your community and truly change the trajectory of someone's life, including your own.

Remember, you are able. You are strong. You are brave. You are courageous. You are a game-changer.

Love,

Megan Richey

## DEAR HER,

Believe. You may look around at your peers, who appear to be richer, prettier, and smarter than you are right now. Please DO NOT let the thoughts that they are in any way better than you because of these things determine your level of self-worth and self-confidence. Nothing in life is as it appears. Stay true to your feelings and remember that another person's opinions about you do not dictate how much success and happiness you are allowed in this life.

Stay present in your everyday journey. When you are at school, focus on each class; when you are at practice, focus on each play. Tomorrow is not promised. Pay more attention to how things make you feel and less attention to the thoughts of the "what ifs."

Your weight does not determine your worth. Be active and choose foods that make you feel good, but the quicker you can separate your self-worth from your jean size, the quicker you can have more time to be a critical thinker, an innovative thinker, and have more fun.

You can do what you want in this world. Setbacks are simply minor bumps in the road. Some of the most successful people have had the most setbacks. Please know that a woman is just as powerful as a man. Please know that a gay woman is just as powerful as a straight man.

The impact you can have on this world is unimaginable. Every day and every encounter are a chance to improve someone's life, as well as your life. Read more books and remember that you have exactly what you need inside of you to do whatever you want to do in this world. The world is yours and you are the director of your life. What scene do you want to be remembered for? You deserve anything in this world.

Always,

Michelle Van Dyke

## DEAR HER,

I see you every day putting in so many hours into your craft though the gym is empty. I hear you when you grunt out of disappointment, cry out of frustration, and self-encourage though no one is around. I feel your pain from all the running, cutting, jumping, banging down low, and dribbling till your arms burn. I completely and wholeheartedly understand you when you've got your hands on your knees breathing hard, wondering if everything you are going through right now is worth it.

You don't know it yet, but all these little things will add up one day. The sacrifices you are making now will pay dividends down the road, should you choose to stay on this path. I tell you now that it will be lonely at times, and you will be tempted to accept mediocrity so that you may "fit in," or worse, quit altogether. There will be times when the people you thought were for you were only there because you are on the same platform, not surpassing. Opportunities such as boyfriends, slumber parties, and other rites of passage for your age group will be missed because of your craft.

I tell you now, do not lose heart. Every drop of sweat, blood, and tears is worth it, because at the end of the day, no one can say that you didn't put in the work or give it your all if you truly have. "Find a way to do it, and get it done" is the mentality needed for you to reach the next stage in your development. You don't need your coaches or your peers to recognize the extra work you put in; that is for you. You also don't need the fancy equipment, the hottest shoes, or even a gym membership to put in work. There is always something you can be doing to be better, faster, and stronger; 'tis the beauty of this sport. There is always something that can be improved.

I say this to you because you need to hear it: for all its worth at the end of the day, I am proud of you for pushing through it. I am proud of you.

Keep the faith,

*Nadia Parker*

144

# DEAR HER,

As I look back on my journey and I reflect on my success and "failures," I want you to know that YOU matter! I want you to know that you are seen and there is no one on this earth that has your gifts or can do what you are able to do. God only created one of you with your gifts, talents and strengths which are unique to only you. Do not feel like you need to be someone else! As you get older, you will be able to find out more what those are, but in the meantime, give 100 percent to everything you do! Give your all to your academics, give your all to every practice and game and give your all to your family and friends. Do not feel that you have to have the answer to everything about yourself, your future or next steps. I promise, that comes if you choose to focus on the present, enjoy it to the fullest and give your all (remember, it is a choice).

I understand that being an athlete can sometimes be very difficult mentally, physically and spiritually, yet I promise that what you learn on the court and field will be lessons you will carry for the rest of your life. I understand the concept of working hard at my job because I learned to work hard in sports. I understand the concept of teamwork because there never was a basket scored that was not the product of an assist, or a game won alone. I understand what it means to get back up after a "failure" or lost game (or even a turnover) because I learned to do it on the court. I understand what it means to respect authority (coaches) and follow orders or advice for the sake of the team and my own growth. As you can see, the lessons you choose to learn in sports and practices will stay with you for the rest of your life and can be implemented in all aspects of your life (work, family, volunteer, etc.). Even if your goal is not to continue to play sports for the rest of your life, you will be grateful you did at this age! Keep grinding through it, because it is worth it! You will be that much more ahead of the game later on!

Lastly, I want you to encourage you to continue to take care of your body physically, mentally, emotionally and spiritually. Being a student-athlete can sometimes be very draining but taking the right steps to take care of your body will help you go farther. A few tips from my end: make sure you are fueling your body with the right nutrition, get enough sleep because it will help you to be able to give your all to everything you do, and take some time to journal and record what you are feeling or going through. I want you to know that you are not alone in this journey! There are many other women that have gone through similar things like you have and understand that it can be hard. With that said, do not be afraid to ask others to help or mentor you to help you reach your goals! Keep fighting, know you are powerful beyond your understanding and know you are beautiful inside and outside! Let your OWN light shine! Do not look to what others are doing (unless it is to learn) and embrace your own journey!

Love,

*Nayelli Casarrubias*

## DEAR HER,

To be an athlete is, in my opinion, like having a super power. There are some things you can do that others can't. You compete on a stage, with an audience, dazzling and uplifting others, sometimes for just a moment, but often for much longer.

And what's in it for you? You learn that you are more powerful than you thought, that you can think and execute under pressure, that you can work together with others, that you can bounce back from a loss. And perhaps most importantly, that you are also a skilled juggler, balancing the balls of school, sports, and relationships high up in the air.

When your glory days are over, your super powers remain! You'll have what it takes to excel in a career because of the self-discipline you've learned. Long hours will be a breeze compared to running suicides till you're ready to puke. A demanding boss will be bearable because of that one coach who was always riding you. That big interview for your dream job won't shake you because the two free throws you made, or that goal you scored, or that base hit you nailed with the game on the line, will pop into your head at just the right time. And if you choose it, you will hold up under the stress of working, marriage and motherhood, because you will remember that you are a master juggler.

I can't tell you how many times I've hit a wall, like the abrupt change in family finances that required my work hours as a sophomore at UC Berkeley to go from 10 per week to 30, or like the grueling 80-hour weeks during the busy season at a huge CPA (accounting) firm; like the grind of graduate school, working, mothering, wife-ing, and care-giving for a sick parent all at once. Every time, that "one-more-rep-even-though-I-can't-feel-my-legs" spirit of the athlete in me, my super power, kicked in and pushed me through!

I'm writing you, my DEAR HER, to remind you that, as the great poet Marianne Williamson, wrote, "You are powerful beyond measure." Keep training, keep competing, and keep showing up! Everything being an athlete has cost you, or taught you, will serve you at every stage of your life, and long after your days of running a mile, or wearing a jersey are gone.

The wins and setbacks of life will look a lot like those of your playing days. Remember your super powers! You will get through it all because the athlete in you has given you proof of your ability to do so!

All the best,

*Pamela Anderson*

# DEAR HER,

As I sit down to write this letter, I start to cry. I don't know why; I guess I've never actually sat down and thought about how sports have directly shaped my life, and I feel strangely emotional when I think about it. Sports have molded me into who I am, they have molded my body, my self-confidence, my mind, my friendships, and I am so STOKED for you that you've found sports. I believe in the pureness of sports. The pureness of when a bat hits a ball in just the right way, those moments that get you off your seat in anticipation of a goal or a bucket, its creative expression, and the most basic form: free play. But it's also about the pureness you find within yourself. The mental game, the toughness game, the courage game, the "am I having fun" game. The "how do I get one percent better every day" game. What do I need to do make my mind sharper and my body stronger?

Sports are all about the individual and the team. You learn to work together, share, and figure out problems as a group. As an individual, sports can take you wonderful places. I am not a professional athlete or even a highly sought-after college athlete. I could never compete at that level, but I am still an athlete. I've continued to pursue my physical fitness and to learn different sports as I age to not only challenge myself, but also to have fun overall, because FUN is what it really is all about. Your definition of fun might be different than mine. You might enjoy putting your body through some pain so you can look back and say "hey, that was fun." That's what we call type 2 fun. It might suck in the moment, but after the fact, that feeling will keep drawing you back, because you feel most alive when you are challenging yourself and feeling a sense of confidence and freedom that you might not get in any other aspect of your life. And there will be failures and missteps, injuries and setbacks, but those are the things that will make you stronger. They will open doors for you that you didn't even know existed, because failure isn't there to knock you down. It is there to lift you up and redirect you so you know you can do better, be better next time, and that that was not your path. Channel your failures and they will drive you, because if you didn't fail, winning or success wouldn't be as exhilarating as it is.

My journey started as a little girl on the playground in New York City, the ultimate concrete jungle. I was an energetic child, always climbing to the top of the monkey bars, running around the park, free-playing all over the place. I went to tennis camps and did gymnastics. I learned to ski and snowboard and sail. In high school, I played field hockey, softball, and ran track. I was a three-sport varsity athlete. I enjoyed the competition, the camaraderie of my teammates, and the confidence I began to build about myself and my body in terms of what it could accomplish when I put my mind to it. I was good, but I wasn't the best, and that's okay. I always gave it my all, the best I could do, and that is the most important thing you can do.

These days will go fast, and I urge you, do not take these days for granted. As they say, hindsight is 20/20, and you may not be thinking about it, but these are the days that you will look back on when you get older, to understand where you came from, why you do the things you do, how you got to where you are today. They will be some of the most difficult days, but also all some of the most rewarding, filled with laughter, excitement, and self- awareness.

In high school, I was not only just an athlete, but also a girl who loved watching and talking sports. I'd take myself to the Bronx and go to Yankee games, catch US Open matches with my mom, ditch class to watch March Madness. Being a female who is an athlete and who loves sports has taken me many places and opened lots of doors. I attended the University of Michigan-Ann Arbor because

I wanted to go to a big school, with an even bigger sports program. As an incoming freshman, I secured season football, basketball, and hockey tickets, and I was so excited to be a Michigan Wolverine. At this point, my dream was to work in sports. If I couldn't be a professional athlete, at least I could be close to the action. I was a Sports Management and Communications major in the School of Kinesiology, where I took classes that ran the gamut from Sports Law and Journalism to Human Anatomy and Nutrition. I pretty much ate, slept, and breathed sports. When I wasn't attending games or studying for my classes, I was taking part in recreational sports. This was a great opportunity to stay fit and to socialize. I played club field hockey, intramural soccer, pick up tennis, and started taking Pilates classes, which opened a completely new door for me. I know that we see on TV and Social Media that being an athlete is a job, a lucrative one, but you do not have to be a professional to be an athlete.

It is important to not take yourself too seriously and that being an athlete can mean that you play sports recreationally and are interested in fitness. Health and Wellness has always played a role in my life. It has always been important to me to be strong so that I can take on any physical challenge that is thrown my way. When I am feeling strong, I am feeling confident, and I feel like I can conquer the world.

I try my best to do my due diligence to eat healthy-ish (I mean, let's be realistic here, French fries and chocolate are my favorite) and get to the gym so that I can continue to take my body to new and exciting places. Pilates and Yoga have helped me strengthen my body and my mind in ways I could never imagine, and I wish I started both those practices at a young age, because they bring out a different type of toughness in me.

When I got to that point in college where everyone asks you, what are you going to do with your life, working in sports was the obvious answer. I had already dedicated my entire life to this passion. During college, I interned with the Detroit Pistons, Major League Baseball Productions, and IMG, testing out which path was mine. Did I want to work in communications for a sports team? Did I want to be a broadcaster or produce videos? Did I want to be an agent? These are all important questions to ask yourself and important things to suss out. You DO NOT have to go down one path; you can try many different ones to see what fits. I had no idea what I wanted to do; all I knew was that I wanted to work in sports.

After college, I ended up getting a job in the Public Relations Department at Major League Baseball's Office of the Commissioner. It was exciting and, to be honest, mundane at the same time. I came in bright-eyed and excited to learn, but came out disillusioned by the sports industry, and that I was childish and naive to think that the pureness of sport is what drove sports: it's not—it's money. I also realized that I am not a desk person. All those years of being an athlete, running around, recreating, made me recognize my bountiful energy, and that I needed more fresh air in my life. I needed to be moving my body, outside, in the fresh air.

I moved from NYC to Vail, Colorado, to work in the ski industry. I wanted to be a ski bum. I was 23, and that decision was the best decision I made in my life at that point. As Yogi Berra once said, "If you see a fork in the road, take it." Being in the mountains and snowboarding a hundred days a year changed the trajectory of my life. I made adventurous friends who were all about getting up early to go shred, hike, or mountain bike. I learned that the mountains and nature can fill you up with so much gratitude and joy, and that all you need to access those feelings are your own two feet. I felt freedom in the form of the wind rushing past my face, my body taking me places I never thought I'd ever go, and a place where I found my creative spirit. I look back fondly on those six years I spent living in the mountains, and I encourage you to follow your intuition. You do not need to rush into a career.

Experience letting your mind and body take you places you never thought you'd go. Say "YES" to those new experiences that scare you a little and will ultimately enrich your life, because that is where change happens. When you find yourself at the edge of your comfort zone, peeking over, asking yourself, "Do I dare?" and oh, you should. My life has been built upon pursuing an active lifestyle. By writing this letter to you, I have fully realized that it has been my life's driving purpose to constantly be moving, feeling strong, and confident within my body. I love feeling strong, like I can do anything. I'm okay not being the best among others, as long as I'm my own best. I'm at my best when I am outside being active, no matter what anyone else is doing. I now live in San Francisco and I work in the outdoor industry in public relations and social media. I was able to finally mesh my love of sports and being outdoors into a career. It didn't happen overnight. It's a journey, a process where you go through many phases to figure out how you can create something for yourself that you are passionate about.

My one constant passion has been sport. Even though at the beginning of my journey I thought I'd be working in "traditional" sports, I still found a niche that affords me the lifestyle I like to lead and working in an industry I am passionate about. The journey of being an athlete is a rewarding one. It definitely comes with ups and downs, but always embrace the good with the bad and don't take it all too seriously, because in the end, it's all about who is having the most fun, who is being their truest self, who is stepping into their power, who is determined to improve themselves that one percent every day. Enjoy the journey, because the journey is the destination.

Sincerely,

*Rachel Friedman*

## DEAR HER,

There's no such thing as failure! Really, it doesn't exist, because the only way you fail is to stop. Kobe taught me that. It took me a long time to believe that and commit to that mentality, but that's completely changed the game for me (someone who was constantly driven by the thrill of success or the fear of failure). To me, losing always felt worse than winning felt good. In other words, I hated to lose more than I loved to win. Now, that still sometimes is the case, but I've learned that both mindsets (loving to win or hating to lose) really limit your growth, because you're focusing on just the outcome. Now for a coach, that's tough, because you're judged by that Win/Loss column. As a teacher and, hopefully, a mentor to my kids, it *has* to be more than just a W or L, because even if you do all the right things, you can still lose, and even if you do all the wrong things, you can still win. It has to be about growth. Did we get better? If so, how can we replicate that? If not, why, and how can we get better next time? I challenge myself and my kids to think like this: "prioritize growth over outcome," and I think that has a lot to do with our success in our current basketball season. Does that mean we're perfect? Far from it!

In fact, I just kicked them out of practice the other day. But to me, that wasn't failure. It sent a message that I needed to be delivered. And they responded by winning the game the next day. Message received. Now does it feel this way just because we won, maybe? I don't really know. But in that moment (when I decided to kick them out of practice the day before a game), I didn't prioritize winning; I prioritized our growth. And whether we won or lost that game, I think we would have grown as a team, because we would have understood what not to do the next time. So, take the risk. Challenge yourself. Don't be afraid to fail. Because yes, the outcome might not turn out the way you want it to, but ultimately you learn from it and you get better. BE RELENT-LESS IN THE PURSUIT OF WHAT MAKES YOU GROW.

Sincerely,

Riki Murakami

## DEAR HER,

Hey, there. It is future you. As I write you now, I'm about to celebrate New Year's Day in the year 2018. A couple of things you should know that might be alarming. Arnold Schwarzenegger was Governor of California for a bit. Pretty much nothing you saw in Back to the Future II came true. We still don't even have jetpacks yet. And I'm pretty sure you've never heard of Donald Trump but ... well, we won't get into that.

Here's what I do want to get into, and this may come as a shock, as well—*You are an athlete.* No, really, you are.

I know you're finding this hard to believe. Especially at this moment, in 1990, during your sophomore year in high school. You're blowing off PE class again. I see you doing what you always do, casually walking around the field with a couple of your friends, out of sight of the teacher, going on and on about this unknown new band you just discovered called the Red Hot Chili Peppers.

But I'm telling you ... *you are an athlete.*

And really, if you think about it, hints were there.

Remember all those years you spent at summer camp? You swam and waterskied almost every day for a month every summer between 1983 and 1988. Remember how you felt the first time you got up on a single waterski? Oh, and there were the countless hours you spent on roller skates when you were young, skating in circles in your garage and around the cul-de-sac while listening to Madonna and the Beastie Boys. You should really pin this one in your mind.

So, yeah. *You are an athlete.* But somewhere along the way, you stopped believing this about yourself. Or maybe you never did.

Growing up, you never really knew what it was like to be a part of a team working together toward a common goal. You were never one of the "cool kids," and maybe you thought sports were only for the popular crowd. You definitely had a hard time with most sports in PE class. Except hockey, for some reason. You killed at that. I feel like that's going to somehow be relevant later.

And now, you struggle to find your place in high school. You moved to a new city shortly before your freshman year, and even as a sophomore, you still don't quite know where you fit in.

You may have spent most of your life convincing yourself that you're not and will never be an athlete, but deep down, you have character traits that will help define you as a leader and a team player. You will discover things you love, and you will pursue them with all your heart. Whether it's writing for the school yearbook or being a super fan of your favorite band (*cough*REDHOTCHILIPEPPERS*cough*), you go all-in.

You'll learn that you have a talent for singing and performing, but it will require you to step on stage and show what you can do. You will discover how rewarding it can be to go outside of your comfort zone to prove your worth and eventually shine.

You're going to find your way soon enough. Not to influence your future too much, but an audition (outside your comfort zone) will lead to a role in the high school production of Bye Bye Birdie (you love singing and performing). You will finally experience what it's like to be a part of a tight-knit, disciplined team working toward a common goal. This will be a bit of a game changer for you.

So how did your high school stage debut help you bring out your inner athlete?

In 2001 (THE FUTURE!), a group of women in Austin, Texas will form a women's roller derby league. These women are not traditional athletes—they will bring a rebellious, punk rock attitude to a full contact sport on roller skates.

In 2003, you will move to Los Angeles. As an effort to meet new people, you will go on this thing called the internet (we can talk about that some other time) and find an ad for an upstart women's roller derby league called the LA Derby Dolls. *I told you to remember the part about roller skating!*

On a November evening shortly before your twenty-ninth birthday, you will go to your first practice by yourself. It will be intimidating and scary, but you will fall in love with it immediately. You will discover this perfect mix of performance and athleticism that makes roller derby the perfect vehicle for you to wake up that long-hibernating athlete inside.

You will play competitive roller derby for over a decade, past your fortieth birthday. You will experience the struggles of losing seasons and the extreme high of carrying a championship trophy on a victory lap. You will learn to embrace and love the discipline of training. You will know the joys and challenges in leadership and learn how to be a great teammate. You will gain confidence that will carry well beyond the competitive arena. It will be life-changing.

Oh, and you'll also pay it forward, helping other people become athletes. Even kids and teens will have access to roller derby, and you'll help teach them how to play. You'll have fleeting moments where you will wish you could have started when you were younger, but it won't bother you for long. You'll realize that your life went exactly the way it was supposed to go. Plus, it turns out there's no upper age limit when it comes to playing sports. You'll continue to fuel your competitive spirit into your forties, and with any luck, well beyond.

So, for now, keep rocking out to the Red Hot Chili Peppers. Keep singing, dancing, performing and going outside of your comfort zone. And keep roller skating any time you get the chance.

All of this will continue to shape you as an athlete. Which you are, by the way.

With love,

*Future You*

aka The Improbable Athlete (Robin Legat)

## DEAR HER,

The fight is worth it. The late nights, dreaded training sessions, three-hour practices, even the tears ... they are all worth it! Being a competitive athlete is challenging. It is scary at times and it pushes your limits. I will never forget a night, early in my athletic journey, when I started crying because my abs were so sore it was too painful to even laugh. But it was nights like these and so many more, when I thought that was it—my coach wasn't being fair, I didn't have the time, I couldn't get any better—when I learned the most. Whatever the excuse might have been, I now know that was my own fear holding me back. It was my fear of not being able to reach the expectations of my coaches. Learning how to overcome self-inflicted fear was one of the most valuable lessons I took away from my athletic journey.

My breakthrough happened at the Yard training center during a session with Leslie. My goal for the summer was to conquer the challenge of a 36-inch box jump. Day after day, week after week, I would miss the goal, until I finally took away what was holding me back. Surprising to most, this barrier had nothing to do with my physical ability. It was all mental. The day I took on the box jump with no fear was the day I cleared the 36 inches that summer. I know this to be true because Leslie said, "Now, look, to prove to you that your brain was holding you back, let's move the box to the other room and see how you do." Once in the other room, I didn't get it on my first couple of tries. I was dumbfounded. A minute ago, I had just cleared the box five times in a row! So again, I MENTALLY took away the barrier and found myself clearing the same 36 inches with a different background.

After this experience, Leslie gave me a book all about fear and the limiting power fear has over us. Many people think that there is nothing good that can come from failure, when in fact failing is one of the most valuable things we can experience. Once I understood that success only came with failure, my mentality completely shifted, for the better. It was the summer after my freshman year in college, and for the first time in my athletic journey, I realized how often I let my own fears stop me from reaching my full potential. In the days, weeks, months, and years following this moment, I played what I think was the best volleyball I played during my entire career. Most people think this is because of the major physical transformations that I made to my body, but

I believe something different. Sure, the physical changes helped me be faster, jump higher, etc., but what was at the root of this change was my mental state. For the first time I approached every rep in practice, every rep in the weight room, and every point in a game without the fear of failing. I stopped trying to predict what would happen if I missed the risky set or couldn't clean that amount of weight. My motto became, "You'll never know if you don't try!"

I started to shift my mentality first with the small things. For example, after my first set, if Leslie asked if I could go up in weight, I would respond with a very confident "Yes," and in my head telling myself, "Oh, yeah! You got this!" Once I started making a habit of this in training sessions, I saw it carrying over to practice and then games. I truly felt confident, strong, and powerful for maybe the first time in my life. I demanded respect in the gym and on the court because I truly believed that I could do anything I set my mind to. Not only did this make me a better player, but it also made me realize the importance of constantly pushing yourself. We should always be trying to achieve something more, because as humans we never stop learning and, therefore, we can always get better.

Even though my volleyball career is technically over, I will always consider myself a competitive athlete. Life is a game. You have opponents who try to bring you down, you face competitions in the workplace, you have bosses, who, like coaches, you may not always agree with, but you have to learn to work for the same goal, and you have family, co-workers, and friends who all become a part of your team. The lessons I learned during my career come up in my day-to-day life, and I am forever grateful for my experience in competitive sports. I would kill to have one more game, but I find myself getting the same joy I got from sports from other things in life. Sure, my goals have shifted from winning a CIF championship to getting my market report out before our firm's competitors, but at the end of the day, I use the same tactics to accomplish my goals. Most importantly, I don't fear failing.

DREAM BIG! FAIL! WORK HARD! It's all worth it!

xoxo,

*Sarah Lucenti*

## DEAR HER,

You are entering a new, exciting, and confusing period in your athletic journey. I couldn't be prouder of you! As you mature in the game and in life, I have a few important keys that will help you.

**Never lose yourself in the game**. As hard as you train and as hard as you work to get to the next level, always remember that there is a person behind the jersey. You have many talents and valuable attributes other than scoring points for your team. It's important to remember that. Your value lies in who you are as an individual, not who you are as a player. All the accolades and awards are fantastic, but the woman that can face herself every day and say "I am awesome because I am alive" won't be held back by anyone. When it's time to hang up your sneakers or cleats, you will know that you can conquer the world. Here's a tip; keep a journal so you can document the things that are important to you. This will come in handy later, trust me.

**How you do anything is how you do everything**. Practice matters. The way you practice is the way you are going to play in the game. You might be the best player on the face of the earth, but you are not too good for practice. If you think about some of the top performers, they get their reps in with the team and on their own. They don't wait for someone to tell them to put up shots, they put up shots because they want to be the best they can be. They also focus on the fundamentals. If you practice the fundamentals and get great at them, all the fancy stuff will make sense when it's time to stunt, lol. This goes double for life after sports.

**If you aren't confident yet, be courageous instead**. Confidence is overrated. Some might say you are building confidence through sport, but I think you are building your ability to be courageous in situations when you aren't confident. The truth is, you will experience fear. Fear is a natural reaction that has kept us alive for millions of years, but it's those that are willing to push forward, even if they aren't confident, that win. If you aren't confident, summon your courage to do the thing anyway. You've got this.

**Consistency is where the MAGIC happens**. I know you look at movies and social media and you see people that seem to have "made it" overnight, but there is always a story of work behind their success. The key to success (which you must define for yourself) is to consistently make progress toward your goals. The person that achieves their dreams is the person that doesn't quit when things get hard. Consistent progress is MAGIC. Pro tip: Learn to fall in love with the journey. It's where the most growth happens.

**Live FULLY and CREATIVELY.** Life is serious, but it's not that serious. During all your pursuits to greatness in sports and in life, always make time for self-expression and activities that bring you joy. There will be times in life where it will seem like things aren't going your way but hold tight to those things that bring a smile to your face and make you laugh. Be the person you want to be and don't worry if people don't understand. You have to live with you. Be kind, empathetic, and compassionate, but live life on your terms.

These are the things I wish I had been told when I was your age. I pray that you grow strong in your sport and even stronger in your WOMANHOOD. Here are my final thoughts. The letters in this book come from women who want to see you succeed. We want you to become woman of integrity, contribution, and have YOUR definition of success. As much as we want that for you, you MUST want it for yourself even more. I want to leave you with something you can say to yourself when you feel "less than" ... I AM EQUIPPED, I AM DESERVING, I AM WORTHY, and I CAN DO THIS!

Peace and Blessings,

*Shannon M. Carlisle*

## DEAR HER,

First of all, I just want to start off by telling you that every-thing will always work out the way it is supposed to. I am just going to share some advice for areas in life from my personal experiences, and the best guideline the Holy Bible. The truth is, the sooner you realize that God has a plan for your life and your light is needed in the world, the less stressed you will be. I know many times it might seem like his plan is shaky, and as if there really isn't a plan at all, but keep your faith in GOD and believe that everything happens for a reason, on his time, and not our own. "For I know the plans I have for you," declares the Lord, "plans to prosper you and not harm you, plans to give you hope and a future." **(Jeremiah 29:11)**

**FAITH:** "For God so loved the world, that he gave his only begotten Son, that whosoever believeth in him should not perish, but have everlasting life. (John 3:16). You may not always understand all the words in the Bible, but you know that you were created for a reason, that you have a purpose in life, you do not know what that purpose is as of now, only God does. If you want to fulfill that purpose and live life to the fullest, continue to learn about Jesus, follow him, live as he did; you will make mistakes and fall short on this roller coaster of life, but get back up and keep trying to live the life he planned for you. It's okay if you get angry at church, religion and don't want to read your Bible. Jesus doesn't care about all of that, he just wants a one-on-one relationship with you; he just wants your heart. It's totally cool and normal if you don't understand why things are happening the way they are, just know that it's not your job or even your right to understand and know everything that God has planned. Your job is to follow him with you heart and be an example for the world. He created all things and gave you all your abilities; therefore, nothing is possible without him. Keep him first in all that you do.

**FAMILY & FRIENDS:** You don't get to choose your family. They are your blood, and the older you get, you will learn to appreciate them. You may not always like them, you may never like them, but you have to love them; make a conscious effort to love them, because you share the same bloodline. Friends will come and go, but the ones that are there with you through the good and the bad, through the rain and the shine, those are called true friends, and if you just have one in this lifetime, you have been extremely blessed. Cherish the time you get to spend with family and friends, because nothing is guaranteed and people change.

**DON'T COMPARE YOURSELF TO OTHERS:** There are billions of people in the world, but there is only one of you. "I praise you because I am fearfully and wonderfully made ..." (Psalms 139:14). So be you, embrace you, love you. Yes, there may be people that are taller than you, skinnier than you, prettier than you, smarter than you or have more money than you. But they will never be YOU. If you try to compare yourself to other people, you will be wasting your time trying to be them and not yourself. You should be your biggest competition; challenge yourself to be the best you every day, but also you should be your biggest fan; praise yourself for the accomplishments you achieve, even if they are small. Remember to be grateful for small things, and bigger things will come to you. The world needs your light, your humor, kindness, intelligence, your laughter and most importantly, your heart. The more you love yourself on the inside, that love will spread to so many on the outside.

**LIFE STRUGGLES:** There are going to be good times in life and there will be bad times in life. Your struggle may be different from someone else's struggle. Unfortunately, life wasn't meant to be easy. You cannot control the uncontrollable, all you can do is control how you respond to these unpleasant circumstances and continue to grow, develop and be a leader for others around you. Just know that God gave the hardest battles to his toughest soldiers. However, you will win the war. The trials you face in life produce perseverance, perseverance produces strength, and strength creates a good character. "And patience, experience; and experience, hope." (Romans 5:4)

**SPORTS:** Play every sport that interests you; play for fun, play competitive, play professionally, put in the work, be disciplined, strive to be the best player, the best athlete you can be. But the minute it stops being fun, it stops being your passion, give it up. At the end of the day, sports are just a game. The world won't end if you miss that shot or lose that game. Don't forget, you will be an athlete for a few years in life, but you will be a human being for the rest of your life. It's better to be remembered as a good player, but an even better person.

**BEAUTY:** Black is beautiful; love your natural hair, your athletic build. Just know that the things that make you beautiful can only come from within; you were already born beautiful everything else is just an additive. It's okay to be a tomboy; athletic women rock and are powerful mentally and physically. Just because you have defined biceps and a six pack doesn't mean you're not feminine. You don't have to fit into society's idea of what beauty is, and what sexy is. True beauty is measured by a woman's smile and her heart.

**RELATIONSHIPS:** Love is Love. You don't have to always know exactly who you like, or what you like, you are free to explore and try new things and change your mind. Don't let others judge you or confine you into a box. However, when the right person comes along and sweeps you off your feet, don't be afraid to open up and let them love you. To love and to be loved is the greatest gift in life. I think the best relationships start as friendships, then becomes something more serious. Enjoy it, it's fun and exciting.

**GENEROSITY:** Love others, as you love yourself. "...Thou shalt love thy neighbor as thyself. There is none other commandment greater than these." (Mark 12:31). This means to treat people how you want to be treated, even if they don't treat you right or deserve it. What goes around comes around, and it is better to do something nice for people and not expect anything in return, especially to strangers. "...It is more blessed to give than to receive" (Acts 20:35). You don't have to be rich to help others. You can give back by donating your time, or volunteering at a shelter. Remember, you came onto this earth with nothing, and you're going to leave it with nothing. You cannot take your riches with you. The best reminder I like is this, Jesus came to the earth to serve not to be served. "Even as the Son of man came not to be ministered unto, but to minister, and to give his life a ransom for many." (Matthew 20:28) So be generous.

*From a disciple, a daughter, a sister, friend and fellow athlete, continued blessings on this journey of life.*

Sincerely,

Shay (Eshaya) Murphy

## DEAR HER,

A letter to myself:

**Mindset**: Change your mindset, baby girl, and change a lot in your life. Understand that your mindset can catapult you further than your wildest imagination, hold you back into the darkest mental prison, and bounce you everywhere in between. You are human; you will visit every one of those places, and you will see your resiliency. You will visit that dark place, feel it, understand it, and how you got there ... but keep it as a short visit and move on. Move on to the middle part, where you find your way out of the dark place, experience life, and explore. Explore places and explore who you are. What do you want? How do you move forward with your goal? Who do you ask to join you on the many journeys you will embark upon?

Please, remember the journeys, the smells, the scents, the visuals, the way you felt emotionally and physically; was your skin kissed by the sun or did a slight breeze brush up against it? Live in the moments and use them as motivation to catapult you to the ultimate plans you have derived from the middle place.

Mindset is where we begin, and moving along in this journey we call life, you will accomplish a lot. Some of your thoughts and imaginations that came from the middle place and into fruition will be epic, others will epically fail. You will go through different seasons; you will grow throughout your life. Different seasons will bring you to different strengths, different views, realizations, some will open your eyes to possibilities unlimited. Others will have you in a fog, but you will get to the other side of it. You will fall, but you will get up, clean your skinned knees, wipe the tears, clean your face, change your clothes, and go at it again, until you get it, relentless. Take different routes until you reach your goals.

Paths will be smooth, rocky, sandy, covered in water, hot as the sun, but will lead to the goals. Keep your motivation, pull from your mental file cabinet and apply your past coping skills to the next adventure. Remember, you will always visit all of these places throughout your life, as long as you keep moving towards a goal.

You have many moments; some are meant to be alone and others with companions. Look to others and uplift them as they will uplift you. Work together, do not tear down the next woman to get ahead, and do not tear down the next woman because it is what society is promoting. Media and society have negatives and positives; keep in the back of your mind "throw out the bath water, but keep the baby," throw out things that have potential damage to you and your mindset. Keep negativity away from your psyche; stop it in its tracks. Politely remove or keep at a distance those that have no cares about your well-being. Learn to say no to that which will take you to a dark place. Walk in your truths. What is inside of you is what affects the outside. Empower yourself, and others, to step up and change their mindset. A formidable force of individual thinkers can be powerful individuals and can come together to accomplish great feats, complementing each other's strengths.

Show the next woman or girl their worth and help them to explore finding themselves, their strengths and capabilities. Enjoy the ability to be an example to the next woman or girl. You began at a certain place and have arrived at this place. You arrived with YOUR MINDSET.

Your mindset will dictate how you see yourself, the "imperfectly perfect person," the "comfortable in your own skin," the "I am not my hair," the "I am woman hear me roar," the "I am doing this for me, not for everyone else," the "uniqueness that is you," the "I will not fit into society's norms," the "I am not an Instagram model, I am unapologetically me," the "No filters," the "take me as I am," the "I am capable of so much more," the "actions speak louder than words." the "Let's do this," the "all or nothing," the "I am beautiful because I am me," and the "I am a movement in myself, but a force when we move together."

Realize you are not one-dimensional. You can be so many things, multifaceted. You can have any career or combination of careers that you choose: a doctor, a coach, a business owner, a teacher, a law enforcement officer, or any other pursuit of your passions. At the same time, you can be a goof ball, light-hearted, carefree, and enjoy simple things like birds, butterflies, nature or ice cream, and walks next to the beach. In conjunction with all of this you can be a mother, an aunt, a friend, a sister. In all of this, always remember to be authentically you.

Your mindset grounds you and strengthens you to stand strong and emerge through a storm with an even greater sense of self. Mindset will help you commit to being a whole person – mind, body and soul – unlike the media and society which steal your soul and leave you feeling lost out in the world.

Your mindset sets your confidence, your motivations, your thoughts on what you believe you can be, your mental strength to face adversity, your physical strength when you feel you cannot go on. Your mindset will change, will help you find the path you wish to travel. Your mindset will help you create how society sees you and not how you conform to society.

Your mindset has brought you to the arrival point where you walk in your purpose, as you are, perfectly imperfect, in your skin, YOU ARE EVERYTHING! And I LOVE YOU!!!

Love,

*Topaz Good*

*The following is a letter from a*
*High School Senior to herself the night*
*before a CHAMPIONSHIP Game:*

## DEAR HER,

It is the day before the CIF Championship game, and I would be lying if I said I am not freaking out. The calming thought between now and tomorrow night is to remember why I play ... is it for that little girl going to numerous parks to find hoops to shoot at, or is it for my mom, sticking by my side through it all and making sure I have had the best opportunities since I have been playing? No matter what the reason, I will go out there and play my hardest for my teammates, for my family, and for that little girl who played for nothing but her love of the game.

*Haley Jones*

# Thoughts from the Convos With Coaches Podcast

On our Convos with Coaches podcast, we asked strong and successful women, "What would you tell a teenage girl or your own younger self about the journey of being your best?"

**Following are excerpts from the "DEAR HER" advice given during our interviews:**

*"Stay the course. We get so caught up in the "right now" and our emotions. I would have relieved so much stress if I had seen the bigger picture, that it is going to be okay in the end. Literally, the world is not going to end ... every experience that you go through, whether good or bad, is kind of like building a house brick by brick. Each experience is another brick for you to build endurance and strength for anything that comes into your life. Have faith. 'For I know the plans I have for you,' declares the Lord. 'Plans to prosper you and not to harm you, plans to give*

*you hope and a future.' If God the Creator has a hope and a future for you, then you gotta know not to worry about the outcome. Just do one step at a time."*– **Shay Murphy**

*"Start sooner, get supported and go after your dreams sooner. I feel more confident by taking action and putting myself out there. No fear of judgement or failure. Remember as a two-year-old, if you want to dress up like a superhero and go to the store, you do! You don't care about what others think and are living free. Get out of your own head and follow that same passion and heart in your life."* – **Amber Bowman**

*"You are strong enough, pretty enough, you are powerful enough to achieve anything you want to achieve. You are also strong enough to stand in a spotlight that is meant only for you. Something special happens when you stand in that spotlight."* – **Cynthia Cooper**

*"Be confident to pursue the goal you want and not the goal somebody else wants for you. Figure out what it is that you want and find a way to achieve what you want, and do not feel like you have to cater to what anyone else wants for you or thinks you should want for you."* – **Kelly Dormandy**

"*Don't stress so much! You got to trust what you create. Look at adversity like an opportunity and don't dwell on it. Problem solve and then show your character. That's how you shine.*"
– **Brittany Gilman**

"*Difficulties and challenges in your life help to develop you. An injury can put you in a different trajectory that you can be fully happy and satisfied in. Just keep swimming and it will be worth it.*" – **Shante Cofield**

"*Know the difference between love and abuse, because sometimes the lines get a little blurry. Be who you are and be okay with who you are, especially in high school. I promise it will work out later. Do the hard work of knowing yourself earlier on in life.*" – **Julia Eyre**

"*Slow down and trust the timing that is happening right now. Be in the day and moment. Enjoy and play have fun. Love yourself and appreciate your body. How beautiful, gorgeous and strong your body is right now. You are perfect the way you are, and do not try to get your worth by what others say. Don't try to be anyone else.*" – **Amber Caudle**

"Go after your dream and goals sooner. Get out of your own way and head and continue to follow that passion and heart. You are going to be very successful in what you put out there. Get focused on something. It may change later in life but pick something."
– **Cary Lee Williams**

"Learn the lesson of the day. Don't seek outside approval from people who are never going to give it to you. Seek guidance and seek lessons from people who are willing to give it to you and who will cheer for you when you are down. The vision you have of yourself may be different in the end than what you thought but keep carving out where and what you want to be in life, eventually you will get there. The hardest part is not to give up. Push through— even when you can't see the end, you are carving your masterpiece." – **Deanna Cordova**

"I wouldn't change any of my struggles, because it has helped make me who I am. Always know how amazing and special you are. Do not judge yourself by what others say and don't compare yourself to others. Be 100 percent okay with who you are, and it is all part of the journey, so enjoy it. Be confident. Never lose sight of the fact that you can do whatever you are willing to put in the work for. Have fun, enjoy, laugh, and don't take yourself too seriously." – **Leslie Trujillo**

"*Stop tripping about how you look. You have to stop comparing yourself to other girls. Get out of your head. Just be you. Turn off the TV and do something (read a book, do some homework, apply yourself). Have confidence in yourself unequivocally, do not allow other people to define if you are doing a good job.*"
– **Kim Jones**

"*Be vulnerable and believe in yourself. All people are just people, treat everyone with respect.*" –**Megan Young**

"*Our immediate reaction is to run from fear ... there is so much to gain in going through discomfort. You learn so much about yourself in being uncomfortable. Get used to fear, befriend it, don't avoid it, but embrace it. Other people's opinion of you is not your business. Stay on your own track and be strong. You do not have to have validation from another.*" – **Allah Mi Basheer**

**SUBSCRIBE to our "*Convos with Coaches*" podcast on iTunes or Stitcher to hear more.**

# Final thoughts to remember...

1. Fail forward.
2. Be coachable.
3. Love yourself.
4. You are loved.
5. You are enough.
6. You are not alone.
7. Enjoy the journey.
8. Be your own hero.
9. Laugh. Cry. Learn.
10. Commit to excellence.
11. Find a way, not an excuse.
12. Gratitude changes everything.
13. There is no such thing as perfect.
14. Your dream is worth fighting for.
15. Do not take yourself too seriously.

16. Honor your words and commitments.

17. Build others up, don't beat them down.

18. Do not let your past dictate your future.

19. Trust in your ability to figure things out.

20. Upgrade your habits to reach your goals.

21. Your struggle will become your strength.

22. Find a mentor and reach out and help others.

23. You are more than a label or physical identity.

24. Focus on the process, be present in the moment.

25. Do not give your power away to another person.

26. Do not play small to make other people feel better.

27. Life is not happening to you, it is happening for you.

28. Don't compare yourself to others, run your own race.

29. You deserve to be treated with respect, value yourself.

30. It is not what you do that matters, it is who you become.

31. Surround yourself with positive and empowering people.

32. Plant powerful seeds and pull the weeds in your thoughts.

33. Do not beat yourself up for your mistakes, learn and grow.

34. Do things that scare you and go beyond your comfort zone.

35. Do things that nurture your spirit and make you come alive.

36. Never forget that you are a miracle, there is no one like you.

37. Take care of yourself physically, emotionally, and spiritually.

38. You are responsible for who you become and your happiness.

39. Find a powerful mantra to say to yourself that gives you strength.

40. You never know what someone is going through, be compassionate.

41. There is nothing weak about asking for help, it is the way of strength.

42. BE You! There is no right way to look, talk, dress, act, or be as a woman.

43. Leave judging others and gossiping alone, you do not need that energy in your life.

44. We are proud of YOU!

# QUOTES WE LOVE:

*"Somewhere behind the athlete you've become and the hours of practice and the coaches who have pushed you is a little girl who fell in love with the game and never looked back... play for her."* – Mia Hamm

*"No matter what you look like or think you look like, you're special, and loved, and perfect just the way you are."* – Ariel Winter

*"You have what it takes to be a victorious, independent, fearless woman."* – Tyra Banks

*"We cannot all succeed when half of us are held back. We call upon our sisters around the world to be brave – to embrace the strength within themselves and realize their full potential."* – Malala Yousafzai

*"And the day came when the risk to remain tight in a bud was more painful than the risk it took to blossom."* - Anaïs Nin

*"I am the master of my fate, I am the captain of my soul."*–from William Ernest Henry, *Invictus*

*"Opportunities are disguised as hard work, so most people don't recognize them."* – Anon

*"All flowers in time bend towards the sun."* – Jeff Buckley

*"When I stand before God at the end of my life, I would hope that I would have not a single bit of talent left and could say 'I used everything you gave me.'"* – Erma Bombeck

*"What lies behind us and what lies before us are small matters compared to what lies within us. And when we bring what is within us out into the world, miracles happen."* – Henry Stanley Haskins

*"Reach high, for stars lie hidden in your soul. Dream deep, for every dream precedes the goal."* – Pamela Vault Starr

*"Success is peace of mind, which is a direct result of self-satisfaction in knowing you made the effort to do your best to become the best you are capable of becoming."* – John Wooden

*"The world needs dreamers and the world needs doers. But above all, the world needs dreamers who do."* -Sarah Ban Breathnach

*"Champions do not become champions when they win the event, but in the hours, weeks, months and years they spend preparing for it. The victorious performance itself is merely the demonstration of their championship character."* - A. Armstrong

"*The way of the Champion is a process of keeping in touch with and attending to your purpose and ultimate possibilities; it is about looking for ways to be the very best you can be. To be less than your very best, even as great as you are, is to settle, to become complacent. The true life of a Champion is a constant searching for and practicing those behaviors that contribute to your growth and development, on or off the field. To be willing to do all that it takes—deep desire—requires the element of suffering, a Zen concept that tells us how adversity is the doorway to enlightenment. To be unwilling to leave your comfort zone and enter into zones of discomfort is to forever be oblivious to how Great you might have become. The cure for complacency in any area of life is commitment of the heart ... A deep desire and willingness to doing all it takes to grow and expand, enabling you to forge ahead through any adversity and suffering.*"

**–*The Way of the Champion Book*,** J. Lynch

# The Woman in the Glass

*When you get what you want as your struggle for self*
*And the world makes you queen for a day,*
*Just go to the mirror and look at yourself,*
*And see what that woman has to say.*

*For it isn't your father or mother or friend*
*Whose judgement upon you must pass;*
*The person whose verdict counts most in your life*
*Is the one staring back from the glass.*

*She's the person to please, never mind all the rest,*
*For she's with you clear up to the end.*
*And you've passed your most dangerous, difficult test*
*If the woman in the glass is your friend.*

*You may fool the whole world down the pathway of life,*

*And get pats on your back as you pass.*

*But your final reward will be heartache and tears*

*If you've cheated the woman in the glass.*

Author: Dale Wimbrow
(original poem- "The Guy in The Glass")

# ACKNOWLEDGEMENTS

Our deepest gratitude to the women who contributed to this book by sharing their lives with us through their letters. We know none of us did this alone. There are many people who have come before us, that walk with us, and that are coming behind us to help us step up in our lives—we thank you!

A special thanks to Nicole Ari Parker for taking the time out of her packed schedule to be a part of this powerful project and write the foreword to this book. We appreciate your journey and who you show up as in all areas of your life. Thank you for lighting the way for so many people.

An artistic appreciation to Lucinda Rudolph for her beautiful sketch on our front cover. Thank you for hearing our vision and bringing it to life. It's perfect!

Thank you to the powerful women that were guests on our podcast and shared their "Dear Her" wisdom with us: Cary Williams, Amber Bowman, Megan Young, Dr. Shante

Cofield (the Movement Maestro), Brittany Gilman, Amber Caudle, Cynthia Cooper, Kelly Dormandy, Shay Murphy, Julia Eyre, and Allah-mi Basheer.

We would like to thank all the people that made financial contributions to help fund this project:

Allison and Ian Kennedy, Eric Fonoimoana, Jake Trujillo, Jackie Kirkwood, Lucenti Family, Margot Farris, Kelly Muniz, Liz Holmes, Lisa Beers, Neal Perlmutter, Pamela Anderson, Michelle Toscano, Danielle Adler, Amber Kivett, Madelyn Tournat, Alvin Valdez, Gavin Rubin, Loreyna Ojeda, Carissa Karner, Aaron Ausmus, Alana Binns, Maureen James, Jeysen Delgado, Adina Wiseman, Alicia Richardson, Cary Williams, and Amber Caudle.

## Leslie Cordova-Trujillo's Acknowledgements:

All thanks to my God who has blessed my journey and this project. I would like to thank my parents, Tim and Sandy Cordova, for putting up with me through my difficult teenage years and always supporting me and my dreams.

AND deep gratitude to my family: my amazing husband, Jake Trujillo, two children, Mateo and Anhelica, and other "son" Alex Garcia. Thank you for inspiring me every day and supporting me on this project and the time it took to create it.

DEAR HER...

Thank you to my amazing sister, Deanna, for always having my back in every area of my life. Thanks for all the work you put in to bring this project to life!

Thanks to Coach Kim Jones for trusting me on this Convos With Coaches journey together.

I am grateful for all the coaches, teammates, and friends I have had throughout my life. A special thanks to Kathy Kolanciewicz and Diane O'Neal for introducing me to great coaching and Strength and Conditioning. I'm especially grateful to all the coaches I have worked with as their Strength and Conditioning Coach and the amazing athletes who have trusted me with their dreams while at Loyola Marymount University, Notre Dame, University of Southern California, The Yard Performance Center, Los Angeles Harbor College, Redondo Union High School, West Torrance High School, Rolling Hills Prep, Mira Costa High School, and Torrance High School. Special thanks to the Popovich family for trusting me with their health and performance.

To my Mastermind family and mentors—Chris Rounds, Mickey Marotti, Tony Rolinski, Lisa Shall, Chris Carlisle, Todd Durkin, Jeremy "Troll" Subin, Rosie Thomas, Kelli Watson, Mary Morissey, Mary McKelvey and Dr. Cobb, thank you for believing in me and guiding me. A special thanks to the current coaches I work with to create Cham-

DEAR HER...

Thank you to my amazing sister, Deanna, for always having my back in every area of my life. Thanks for all the work you put in to bring this project to life!

Thanks to Coach Kim Jones for trusting me on this Convos With Coaches journey together.

I am grateful for all the coaches, teammates, and friends I have had throughout my life. A special thanks to Kathy Kolanciewicz and Diane O'Neal for introducing me to great coaching and Strength and Conditioning. I'm especially grateful to all the coaches I have worked with as their Strength and Conditioning Coach and the amazing athletes who have trusted me with their dreams while at Loyola Marymount University, Notre Dame, University of Southern California, The Yard Performance Center, Los Angeles Harbor College, Redondo Union High School, West Torrance High School, Rolling Hills Prep, Mira Costa High School, and Torrance High School. Special thanks to the Popovich family for trusting me with their health and performance.

To my Mastermind family and mentors—Chris Rounds, Mickey Marotti, Tony Rolinski, Lisa Shall, Chris Carlisle, Todd Durkin, Jeremy "Troll" Subin, Rosie Thomas, Kelli Watson, Mary Morissey, Mary McKelvey and Dr. Cobb, thank you for believing in me and guiding me. A special thanks to the current coaches I work with to create Cham-

203

pionship teams in sports and life: Nabeel Barakat, Dean Dowty, Marcelo Enriquez, Lynn Flanagan, Riki Murakami, Lindz Aiko, Neal Perlmutter, and Sammy Brittain.

A special thanks to my Grandma Mary and our life mentor, Mary Louise Romero-Betancourt, for showing us how to live in joy! Thanks to our family members who have supported our journey.

Special thanks to Lilly Hodges for rekindling this idea within me.

I also am grateful for women who I have never met, but who helped me through difficult times in my life through their music and life journey: Mary J. Blige, India Arie, Mary Mary, and Jennifer Lopez. Music is a powerful healer just like the words of these letters...

## Deanna Cordova's Acknowledgements:

From when I was very young, I always knew sports would play an important role in my life; I just never realized how they would shape my entire life, so I'd like to begin by thanking anyone I ever played alongside, played against, was coached by, coached, who cheered me on, and who challenged me to do more; thank you.

I would like to thank my parents, who encouraged my sister and me to play as many sports as possible, who drove us to and from practices and games, and who cheered for us at all of our games.

Thank you to my sister who taught me the importance of being a good teammate, who always had/has my back, and who encourages me to try new things, even—or especially, when—they scare me. To my nephew, Mateo, and my niece, Anhelica, thank you for making me want to be a better person.

My first mentor in life, and probably the best person I have met, Mary Louise Romero, thank you for teaching me to always be a good human first and everything else will fall into place.

My college teammates, who are my family and will always be family, thank you for always cheering me on.

Thank you to Coach Drake, who gave me the opportunity to coach on his staff for many years, and who taught me the importance in believing in others to reach a goal.

To Mike Williams, my mentor, boss, and friend, who passed away too soon, thank you for instilling in me a positive approach to life, a relentless work ethic, confidence to succeed in the fitness industry, but mostly for teaching me to appreciate the good with the bad.

To all my clients who have stuck with me since day one, I would not be who I am without you. I can't thank you enough for your support and encouragement through the years.

To my Cali, Seattle, New Mex, DC people, thanks for loving me, encouraging me, and making me laugh through the tough times and cheering me on through the good times.

Thank you to everyone who took time to write their story to help encourage our next generation of athletes to strive for greatness. 81818.

## Kimberly Jones' Acknowledgements:

Thank you to my Mom and Dad, George and Janice Jones for instilling the discipline, structure and mature mindset required to be respected and successful in this world.

To my older brothers George, Eric and Tim for providing a competitive environment during our backyard scrimmages. You instilled the fight in me that I needed to thrive in a male-dominated profession.

To my mentors Nancy O'Sullivan and Daniel Kohn. Thank you for your trust, patience and support throughout my journey in this crazy athletic world. I would not be the coach I am today if it wasn't for the opportunities you both gave me to grow, mature, and excel.

Nate Fernley, thank you for being you and reflecting what it means to do what's right in this world ... even when it's not easy. I am forever grateful for your spiritual guidance, insight, encouragement, and comedic timing. Even though you don't lift, I still respect you!

Leslie Cordova-Trujillo, you are my spiritual sensei! You always know the right thing to say. Your energy and positivity are contagious! Your re-entry into my life was not a coincidence. The Universe blessed me with your presence and continues to every day. I have a ton of respect for you as a person, wife, coach, mother, mentor and business partner. Convos with Coaches is just the beginning of our reach. We are going to change the world, change the game and change the way women are perceived in the performance world.

12
22

29207459R00126

Made in the USA
San Bernardino, CA
12 March 2019